# ¡VEO TEXTURAS DE

# PELA

por Jenna Lee Gleisner

# TABLA DE CONTENIDO

# PALABRAS A SABER

claro

esponjado

moteado

oscuro

pelaje

rayado

# PELAJES

pelaje

**Yo veo un pelaje.**

3

**Veo un pelaje oscuro.**

**Veo un pelaje claro.**

mota ······▶

**Veo un pelaje moteado.**

raya

**Veo un pelaje rayado.**

**Veo un pelaje largo.**

¡Veo un pelaje esponjado!

# ¡REPASEMOS!

Los mamíferos tienen pelaje. El pelaje mantiene a los animales a salvo y calientes. ¿Qué tipos de pelajes ves abajo?

# ÍNDICE

# Allyson Gof...

# FLAVOURS

**Photographs by Sally Tagg**

Hodder Moa Beckett

**National Library of New Zealand Cataloguing-in-Publication Data**

Gofton, Allyson.
Flavours / Allyson Gofton ; photographs by Sally Tagg. 1st ed.
Includes index.
ISBN 1-86958-982-3
1. Cookery. I. Tagg, Sally. II. Next (Auckland) III. Title.
641.5—dc 21

Text © Allyson Gofton 2003
Photographs © Sally Tagg 2003
Photographs on pages 36–37, 48–51, 70–71, 91, 98–99 © Alan Gillard 2003
Design and format © Hodder Moa Beckett Publishers Ltd 2003

Published in 2003 by Hodder Moa Beckett Publishers Ltd
[a member of the Hodder Headline Group]
4 Whetu Place, Mairangi Bay
Auckland, New Zealand

Printed through Imago Productions, Thailand

# Acknowledgements

A very big thank you to the following people for keeping me up to date with new products to market and for enjoying my enthusiasm for food and cooking:

Jacqui and Phyl Dixon of Sabato, importers of fine Italian and Spanish foods, along with specialty New Zealand products like verjuice, as well as French Valhrona chocolates. You'll find them at 57 Normanby Road, Mt Eden, Auckland and there's always a coffee on offer if you have time to browse. Phone 0800 SABATO or 09 630 8751. Their products can be ordered online at www.sabato.co.nz

Ian Sinclair, Nicole Honiss, Heather Robins and the team at Pepperama. Just around the corner from Sabato, you'll find all things chilli and real Southern Cooking (USA). The shelves are packed with hard-to-find chillies, tomatillos and hot hot hot sauces! The team will make you welcome at 39 Boston Road, Mt Eden, Auckland or phone 0800 424 454. Their product list can be viewed at www.pepperama.co.nz

Marc McDonough and Diane Dolan and their staff at Zarbo Deli. If you have time for a break, nip down to the deli and café on Morrow Street in Newmarket, Auckland for the best latte and peruse the shelves laden with the most wonderful selection of specialist pantry ingredients. There are walnut, almond or hazelnut oils; spices, whole and ground, such as sumac, Sichuan peppercorns or saffron, which keep company with fresh breads, amazing cheeses and dried pulses. Contact them on 09 520 2721. Their products can be ordered online at www.zarbo.co.nz

José Hernandez and his staff at Eurowine, Auckland. They import the finest sherries and ports, including Graham's ports and Lustau sherries. They will direct you to a supplier in your area. Phone 09 636 4045.

Thank you to Liz Parker for allowing me the pages in *Next* magazine to indulge my passion for many wonderful flavours, Sally Tagg for her great photographs and food styling, Alan Gillard for his photographs, and colleague and friend Ann Boardman for her ideas when I needed time out.

And a special thanks to 'spice guru' and friend Ian Hemphill in Australia, whose advice and knowledge is always at the end of an email for me. If you love herbs and spices, his book *Spice Notes* (Macmillan, 2000) is a must in your library.

# Contents

# Introduction

Some years ago, *Next* magazine editor Liz Parker and myself were keen to extend our food section in the magazine. We wanted the additional pages to provide information on essential flavourings that were either new to the market or those that hide on our back shelves or in our gardens and needed bringing to life. Well-known floral photographer Sally Tagg was asked to lend her creative hand to this section's photographs and many times we gained inspiration from Sally's garden for the food photography.

The new column 'Flavour Givers' was about those ingredients that bring food to life or are an essential in creating an authentic dish. It has been wonderful to play with these flavours and to be able to dream up new ways of using them as well as thinking about what our *Next* readers would be likely to try a new flavour in.

We never imagined for one moment that this column would be so incredibly popular and after five years would provide enough material for this wonderful book: *Flavours*.

I now have many favourites: Palm Sugar and Lime Banana Loaf, inspired from a trip to Bali; Lemon Balm Jelly, just wonderful on a summer's day; Seafood Paella, gently scented with saffron and one of my favourite dishes for entertaining; Autumn Mashed Potatoes prepared from the best starchy potatoes with New Zealand pressed walnut oil becomes an exceptional mash; the mellow Prawns in Sweet Hot Curry with the magical souring ingredient tamarind, which balances all the flavour and spices of Indian curries so well; and the fresh-tasting Salmon and Prawn Fish Cakes uplifted by the strongly citrus-scented kaffir lime leaves.

I hope you enjoy experimenting with the flavours in this book as much as I did. Use your imagination: the possibilities are endless.

Happy cooking!

*Allyson*

# Angostura bitters

There's more to Angostura bitters than pink gin and drinks of bitters, lime and soda. Only a few shakes will weave magic on your dishes and leave guests speculating about the mysterious underlying flavour. The Angostura bitters bottle holds a wondrous blend of tropical spices, herbs and plants and is always to be found in my pantry as I find it so useful.

Angostura bitters was created by German doctor Johann Seigert who, in 1824, blended a 'medicine' to bring relief to his patients fighting in Venezuela against the Spanish throne. His home of Angostura on the Orinoco River, where he dispensed his medicine to sailors from all over the world, was to eventually become the name of his aromatic bitters.

## Bitters and rockmelon sorbet

³/₄ cup sugar
¹/₄ cup water
1 large ripe rockmelon, about 1 kg
2 tblsp Angostura bitters
3 tblsp lemon juice

Place the sugar and water in a saucepan and stir over a low heat until the sugar has dissolved. Cool thoroughly.

Cut the rockmelon in half and scoop out the seeds. Scoop the flesh into a food processor and process until smooth. You should have about 2 cups of fruit purée.

Stir together the melon purée, Angostura bitters, lemon juice and the sugar syrup.

### By hand
Place in a deep, lidded freezer-proof container and freeze for about 2 hours until the mixture becomes slushy. Remove from the freezer and beat with a whisk or fork to break up the crystals. Return mixture to the freezer. Repeat this twice more to ensure that the sorbet forms small even crystals resulting in a smooth end product.

### In an ice-cream machine
Transfer to an ice-cream maker and process as per manufacturer's instructions until the mixture is smooth and almost frozen. Transfer to a 3-cup-capacity lidded freezer-proof container, seal and place in the freezer. Use within 4–5 days.

### To serve
Scoop or spoon the sorbet into glasses and serve with a fresh fruit salad.

**Serves 6**

## Tips and ideas
- Flavour a coconut custard or mascarpone cream with Angostura bitters and serve with summer fruit.
- Toss strawberries with Angostura bitters and sugar and marinate for 20 minutes.
- Flavour shortbread with Angostura bitters and lemon rind. Roll thinly and serve to accompany fruit in summer.
- Flavour a banana, sultana or coconut cake with several good dashes in place of vanilla essence.
- Flavour a gravy for pork with orange rind and a few decent splashes of Angostura bitters.
- Use it to make a marinade together with honey, lemon and orange juice. Pour over chicken breasts before baking them.
- Have a southern chicken and rice jambalaya flavoured with Angostura bitters.
- Toss fresh crabmeat with a mayonnaise flavoured with chilli, lime rind, garlic, chives and Angostura bitters.
- For a refreshing drink, try Angostura bitters mixed with cranberry and soda.
- Add a few dashes to a spicy tomato salsa to partner barbecued steak.

# Avocado oil

Avocado oil, with its rich green colour, luscious flavour and smooth texture, is wonderful to have on hand in the kitchen. A completely local product, avocado oil seems to have arrived on our market with gusto, and now it's also available in two scented varieties: lemon and rosemary and chilli with red pepper.

The oil, primarily from the Hass avocado variety, is first collected from ripe fruit by cold pressing. It is then passed through a centrifuge to remove solids and moisture.

Bottled in distinctive dark green glass to help keep out damaging light, the unopened oil will stay stable for up to two years. Once opened, like any oil, it should be kept from heat or light and used within a reasonable time.

## Avocado oil, fruit and nut cake

*Mellow avocado oil is wonderful used in this no-fuss cake that's loaded with mild, dried fruits such as figs and prunes, studded with chopped walnuts and then spiked with spices.*

> 2 oranges
> 1 cup chopped dried prunes and/or figs
> ¼ cup chopped nuts, such as walnuts or almonds
> ¼ cup manuka or rewarewa honey
> ½ cup brown sugar
> ¾ cup avocado oil
> 2 eggs
> 2 tsp vanilla essence
> 1 cup plain flour
> 1 tblsp baking powder
> 2 tsp mixed spice
> 1 cup wholemeal flour
> ¾ cup wheatgerm

Grate the rind from the oranges. Cut away the white pith and finely dice the flesh.

In a bowl, mix together the orange rind and flesh, prunes and/or figs, nuts, honey, brown sugar, avocado oil, eggs and vanilla essence. Beat together with a wooden spoon.

Sift plain flour, baking powder and mixed spice and fold into the wet ingredients with the wholemeal flour and wheatgerm.

Turn into a well-greased and paper-lined 20 cm round cake tin.

Bake at 180°C for 50–60 minutes or until an inserted skewer comes out clean. Cool in the tin. Top with orange icing and walnuts and orange rind, if wished.

**Makes a 20 cm round cake**

# Balsamic vinegar

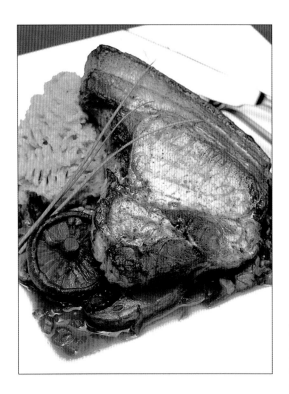

Don't be fooled by the plethora of inexpensive balsamic vinegars that line our shop shelves — most are not the real thing. Instead, it's worth investing in Aceto Balsamico Tradizionale di Modena — the true liquid gold that has uses far beyond the ubiquitous virgin olive oil and balsamic dressing.

Balsamic (which means 'health giving') vinegar is handcrafted in the Emilio-Romagna region of northern Italy. Fresh juice, called 'must', from the Trebbiano grape is simmered slowly until it is reduced to about half or one-third of its volume. Now quite thick and syrupy, it is barrelled with a small amount of old vinegar and a 'vinegar mother' is added to initiate the process of fermentation and acidification.

Thus the 'must' begins its long, slow journey from a coarse wine to a gentle vinegar. There are more than a few years in between — quality balsamic requires passion and patience.

Over the ensuing years or decades (in the case of the finest quality), the vinegar reduces due to evaporation. As this occurs, it is decanted into smaller barrels through a range of different woods — cherry, chestnut, oak and juniper. Each imparts its own essential character. Not unlike the making of sherry, with each transition to a different barrel, a little of the old vinegar remains so that there is a blending with the new.

To be labelled Aceto Balsamico Tradizionale di Modena, the vinegar must be at least 12 years old and approved by the governing body.

True balsamic vinegar is delicious, even sensuous. Rich, sweet and with a velvety texture, use it to enhance foods all year round. Be bold and move away from the tomatoes, basil and balsamic and you'll find it adds a great taste sensation to your cooking. Or mix 1 teaspoonful with a little warm water and drink in the morning as a health restorative.

## Pork with mushroom and balsamic sauce

1 cup chicken stock
15 grams dried porcini mushrooms
4 pork loin chops, rind removed
1 tblsp oil
25 grams butter
1 small onion, finely diced
1 tsp minced fresh garlic
4–6 portobello mushrooms, thickly sliced
4–6 shiitake mushrooms, stems trimmed only
2–4 tblsp finest quality balsamic vinegar

Pour the stock over the porcini mushrooms and set aside.
Pan-fry the pork chops in the hot oil until just tender. Set aside and keep warm.
Add the butter, onion and garlic to the pan and stir over a low heat for 2–3 minutes.
Add the portobello and shiitake mushrooms and cook a further 5 minutes.
Stir in the porcini mushrooms and stock. Simmer until reduced to 1/2 cup.
Stir in pepper to season and the balsamic vinegar.
Serve over the pork chops with plenty of mashed sweet potatoes.

**Serves 4**

# Basil

Nothing compares with summer's first crop of basil. Its large, green, intensely aniseed-flavoured leaves are best late in the season, having had plenty of sunshine and water. And while some may prefer it in pesto, or for turning summer's tomatoes into a meal from heaven, I enjoy it best in this Asian pesto, perfect for marinating chicken, fish or shellfish in for barbecuing over summer.

## Chicken in Asian pesto

1½–2 cups loosely packed basil leaves
2 cloves garlic, crushed and peeled
1 tsp grated fresh ginger
¼ cup pinenuts
1–2 red chillies, deseeded
1 tsp sesame oil
½ cup good peanut oil
1 tsp brown sugar
1 tblsp chopped fresh coriander
pinch of salt
4 single chicken breasts

Put all ingredients (except for the chicken) into a food processor and process until the mixture forms a smooth paste. Add a little more peanut oil if you have to.

Toss chicken breasts in the mixture and marinate in a covered container in the fridge for 2 hours or overnight. The longer you leave it, the more intense the flavour.

Barbecue on a well-oiled medium to hot grill plate until cooked. Do not over-cook on too high a heat, as you will burn the chicken. Allow about 20 minutes cooking time, turning once. Serve warm with a cold salad topped with lime juice or a dash of vinaigrette.

**Serves 4**

## Tips and ideas

- Toast slices of ciabatta bread and drizzle with olive oil. Arrange a slice of juicy red tomato on top and a leaf of basil.
- Toss chopped basil leaves, a little olive oil and parmesan cheese through freshly cooked spaghetti.
- Finely slice basil and mix with softened butter and a little grated lemon rind. Roll into a cylinder and keep well wrapped in the refrigerator. Add a slice to steamed summer vegetables or place on top of a piece of tender grilled steak or fish.
- Add panache to a tossed salad with baby basil leaves or shredded large leaves. Add when tossing the dressing through.
- If you like tripe, try it with a simple sauce of cream, basil pesto (available from supermarkets) and a little grated parmesan.
- Sprinkle chopped fresh basil over a hot pizza. It will greatly improve the final flavour and look.
- Cut potatoes or pumpkin into large chunks and bake in the oven drizzled with a dash of oil and with a chopped onion. Cook until well browned then toss through plenty of basil, a few sliced dried tomatoes, lots of pepper and salt and a dash of vinaigrette. Serve warm.

# Bay leaves

Bay leaves have a distinguished past. The herb's official botanical name, *Laurus nobilis*, translates as laurel (or wreath) and so it was in ancient times that the herb was the laurel with which victorious warriors, sportsmen and poets were crowned.

Aside from its noble history, the bay leaf offers a warm, distinctive and even a sweet flavour in cooking, bringing a roundness to many dishes.

The flavour of bay leaves actually improves with drying, diffusing the slightly bitter notes in the fresh plant. Be cautious when using bay leaves — too many and the flavour will be overpowering. And always remember to remove them before serving the food to your guests. For this reason it is best to use whole leaves — they are easier to find.

The traditional bouquet garni, essential in soups, stocks and casseroles, is made from a bay leaf with a few sprigs of thyme and parsley stalks.

To dry bay leaves, cut stems of leaves from the tree during the day when no dew is left and lie them flat in a dark place. Once dried, store away from light and heat in a dry, sealed container. Kept this way, they will last for two to three years.

When buying fresh bay leaves, make sure they are shiny and green, without blemishes. Dry bay leaves should have a deep green colour, without yellowing.

While bay trees seem to be an expensive purchase, they are long-living and grow to remarkable heights — they make great hedges and topiaries.

## Moghul chicken kebabs

*Bay leaves are essential for the garam masala spice mix used to marinate the chicken in this recipe. Their warm, spicy flavour is further imparted into the chicken by skewering the leaves between the chicken pieces on the kebabs. Brushing the kebabs with egg mix during cooking gives a crusty coating, a technique I learnt on a recent trip to Delhi.*

### Spice mix
        3 dried bay leaves
        1/2 cinnamon stick
        3 tblsp cumin seeds
        2 tblsp coriander seeds
        1 1/2 tblsp whole black peppercorns
        1 tblsp cardamom seeds
        1 tblsp whole cloves
        1 heaped tblsp blade mace
        1 heaped tsp ground turmeric

### Chicken
        8 boneless chicken thighs
        1 cup thick plain yoghurt
        3 tblsp spice mix
        about 12 fresh or dry bay leaves
        1 egg

Crumble the bay leaves and place in a spice or coffee mill with the cinnamon stick. Add the remaining spices to a hot frying pan and cook over a moderate heat for about 2 minutes, until the spices are fragrant but not burnt. Shake pan regularly so that they toast evenly. Cool. Add the toasted spices to the mill together with the turmeric and process until the mixture is fine. Store in an airtight container.

Cut the chicken thighs in half and place in a bowl with the yoghurt and spice mix. Stir to coat evenly. Cover and refrigerate chicken for 4 hours or overnight.

Thread chicken pieces evenly on to 4 metal skewers, placing a bay leaf at regular intervals. Reserve any yoghurt mix.

Place on a foil-lined baking tray and brush with melted butter. Fan-grill at 200°C for 15 minutes.

Beat the egg with 2 tablespoons reserved yoghurt mix and brush this onto the kebabs 3 times during the last 5–6 minutes of cooking.

Serve the kebabs hot on boiled rice with a salad of your choice.

**Serves 4–6**

# Capers

Love them or hate them, you cannot enjoy a tartare sauce without capers. These small, unopened flower buds come from a bush native to the Middle East. Not generally eaten fresh, capers are usually pickled or salted, where their acidic, salty flavour evolves. The buds are picked at their optimum, usually daily. They are then left to wilt in the sun before being preserved in a heavily salted wine vinegar. Alternatively, they are dry-salted and these need to be well rinsed before eating. Caperberries are the pickled fruit of the bush and are meatier in flavour and texture than capers. They make a super garnish. Caper flowers are also available pickled and preserved in olive oil. Try these with fresh cheese on an antipasto platter.

## Goats' cheese, pear and caper pies

*The spicy, salty and unique flavour of capers adds piquancy to the wonderful pear and goats' cheese combination.*

### Rich cheese pastry
> 2 cups flour
> ½ tsp salt
> 200 grams butter, chilled and diced
> 1½ cups finely grated cheddar or tasty cheese
> 2–3 tblsp chilled water

### Filling
> 3 tblsp butter
> 3 pears, peeled and diced
> 4 tblsp caster sugar
> 2 tblsp chopped capers
> 200 grams goats' milk fromage frais (or cows' milk fromage frais)
> 2 egg yolks
> grated rind of 1 lemon
> 200 grams Kapiti Chèvre Tihi, diced

Put the flour, salt, butter and cheese into a food processor and process until the mixture looks like crumbs. Pulse in sufficient chilled water until the mixture forms small, moist balls of dough. Turn out and bring together. Wrap in greaseproof paper and refrigerate for 1 hour before using.

Meanwhile, make the filling. Melt the butter in a frying pan, then add the diced pears and cook until they are golden and tender. Add the sugar and cook until it melts and begins to caramelise. Stir in the capers. Cool.

Beat the fromage frais, egg yolks and lemon rind until smooth. Stir in the pears with any cooking juices and the diced Chèvre Tihi.

Roll out two-thirds of the pastry and use to line 4 x 14 cm flan tins. Spoon an equal amount of filling in each. Roll out the remaining pastry and cut into 4 rounds large enough to cover the pies. Press edges together firmly to seal.

Bake at 190°C for 30–35 minutes until well browned.

Serve the pies while warm. Drizzle with olive oil (lemon-scented is good here), capers and chopped parsley.

**Makes 4 small pies**

### Cook's note
These tarts can be made 1–2 days in advance and reheated for 15 minutes in a 180°C oven.

Look for Chèvre de Bellay, an imported goats' fromage frais, in supermarket specialty cheese sections. If you can't find it, use cows' fromage frais.

# Caraway seeds

Caraway is a remarkable spice. While we probably know the warm, full-bodied and rather earthy flavour of its seeds from foods like rye bread, seedcake or drinks such as schnapps or kümmel, it is also upfront with mint and eucalyptus notes — which we find in mouthwashes and toothpastes.

It is also a great spice to cook with and, in the fiery hot Tunisian paste harissa, toasted caraway seeds bring both warmth and freshness to the heat of the chillies. Normally harissa is prepared from dried red chillies, spices, garlic, salt and oil and it can be blisteringly hot. I've cooled it off a little in the recipe below and added sweet, roasted red peppers and mellow roasted garlic for a more gentle flavour. In another version, I've paired green chillies with oodles of summer herbs.

## Green harissa

> 1 tblsp caraway seeds
> 2 tsp coriander seeds
> 1 tsp cumin seeds
> 125 grams large green chillies, deseeded
> 2 cups Italian parsley leaves
> 2 cups coriander leaves
> 1/2 cup fresh mint leaves
> 2 tsp minced fresh garlic
> 1 tsp salt
> 1/4–1/2 cup oil (olive or walnut)

Toast the caraway, coriander and cumin seeds in a dry frying pan over a moderate heat until lightly toasted. Cool then grind roughly in a mortar and pestle or a spice/coffee mill.

Into a food processor, put ground spices, chillies, parsley, fresh coriander, mint, garlic, salt and oil. Process until smooth.

Bottle in 2 x 1/2-cup sterilised jars. Seal and label. Keep refrigerated and use within 1 month.

**Makes 1 1/2 cups**

## Red harissa

> 1 bulb garlic, roasted
> 2 large red peppers, halved and deseeded
> 2 x 20 gram packets dried red chillies
> 2 tblsp caraway seeds
> 1 tblsp each coriander and cumin seeds
> 1/2 tblsp salt
> 1/2 cup olive oil

Wrap garlic in foil and roast at 180°C for 1 hour or until tender. Grill the red peppers until blackened. Cool and peel. Pour boiling water over the red chillies and leave them to soak for 10 minutes. Drain well.

Toast the caraway, coriander and cumin seeds in a dry frying pan over a moderate heat until lightly toasted. Cool, then put all the ingredients except the olive oil in a food processor and process until coarsely chopped. Add the oil down the feed tube until it has been incorporated and you have thick red paste. Transfer into dry sterilised jars. Seal and keep refrigerated. Use within 1 month.

**Makes 1 1/2 cups**

## Tips and ideas

- Caraway seeds lose their flavour quickly as their highly volatile oil will dissipate quickly. So buy little and often and keep in an airtight container away from the light, heat and humidity.
- The seeds have better flavour if they are lightly toasted before using.
- Add ground, toasted seeds to Indian curries.
- Sprinkle toasted seeds over apples pan-fried in butter to accompany pork sausages or roast pork.
- Caraway balances richness, so add it to a stuffing for roast pork. It will aid the digestion.
- Add a little toasted and roughly ground caraway to bread. Especially nice if you add grated tasty cheddar cheese or a blue cheese as well.
- Make a delicious Liptauer-style cheese spread by blending ricotta with softened butter, salt, paprika, dry mustard, chives and caraway seeds. Great with crackers over summer.

# Cardamom

In ancient times cardamom was one of the most highly-prized spices in the world and among its more historical uses, was used in witches' love potions, a perfume for the ladies of Rome, and was an essential medicine for Ayurvedic healers.

The three-sided plump green pods of cardamom, called the Queen of Spices in India, encase black seeds which can be used whole or ground. With lemon and ginger notes, cardamom is a delightful spice to have in your cupboard.

## Apple and cardamom tarte tatin

**400 gram packet shortcrust pastry**
**1 tsp ground cardamom**
**50 grams butter**
**¼ cup brown sugar**
**grated rind of 1 lemon**
**1–2 tsp cardamom seeds (or 1 tsp ground cardamom)**
**3 cooking apples**

Defrost pastry and lightly knead on a lightly floured board. Sprinkle over the ground cardamom, then knead into pastry. Wrap in plastic wrap and refrigerate until required.

Heat butter in a deep 22–24 cm ovenproof frying pan. Sprinkle over the brown sugar, lemon rind and cardamom seeds.

Peel, quarter and core the apples, then arrange them in the frying pan in a ring around the edge. Fill the centre firmly with one or two apple quarters.

Roll out pastry on a floured board so that it will cover the apples. Tuck edges around apples. Bake at 190°C for 25 minutes. Stand for 5 minutes before inverting onto a serving platter. Serve with whipped cream and garnish with lemon rind, if wished.

**Serves 6**

## Tips and ideas
- Add a couple of crushed pods to pilaf or boiled rice when cooking.
- Apples, pears and nashi improve in flavour when cooked with cardamom.
- Cardamom is regarded as an aphrodisiac and also aids indigestion.
- Crush seeds and add to a bath to invigorate the spirit.
- Sprinkle the spice in a curry to add sweetness.
- Add it to pastries, muffins and biscuits.
- Add ground cardamom when making a fruit loaf — delicious.
- Add ground cardamom to butter with a smidgen of sugar; use to top a muffin.

# Cinnamon

Possibly one of our oldest spices, fragrant cinnamon makes a gentle addition to baking. Cinnamon is prepared from the inside layer (just under the bark) of a tropical tree. The woody spice is peeled into wafer-thin strips that are rolled together and dried out of the sun to become the quills we buy. When purchasing, check to see you really are getting cinnamon. Sometimes cassia — a relation from Asia — is sold instead. Cassia quills are darker and coarser and have a more bitter flavour.

Keep both cinnamon quills and the ground spice in an airtight container. Whole spices will last two to three years, while the ground should be used within 18 months.

## Cinnamon spice cookies

250 grams butter
1 cup caster sugar
1/4 cup golden syrup
1 tblsp liquid honey
2 tsp ground cinnamon
1 tsp ground cardamom
1 tsp ground ginger
1/2 tsp baking soda
1 tblsp water
3 1/2 cups flour
1 tsp salt

Put the butter, caster sugar, golden syrup, honey, ground cinnamon, cardamom and ginger into a saucepan and stir gently over a moderate heat until the butter and sugar have melted. Bring to the boil and then remove from the heat.

Dissolve the baking soda in the water and stir into the butter mixture. Cool for 10 minutes. Sift the flour and salt into a large bowl and make a well in the centre.

Pour in the butter mixture. Using a wooden spoon, mix to a warm, pliable dough. Turn out onto a floured board and knead lightly.

To make the mixture into biscuits, you can:

**a)** Divide dough in half and roll each half into a log about 3 cm diameter. Cover with plastic wrap and refrigerate for 4 hours or until very firm. Cut logs into 0.5 cm slices and place onto a greased baking tray. Bake at 180°C for 12–15 minutes until a deep golden brown, but not burnt. Cool on a cake rack. Store in an airtight container.

**b)** Wrap mixture in baking paper or plastic wrap and refrigerate for 2–3 hours until firm. Roll out, cut in shapes. Bake as above.

**c)** Wrap mixture in baking paper or plastic wrap and refrigerate for 2–3 hours until firm. Press small amounts of dough into wooden moulds, such as the traditional ones for speculaas. Turn onto baking paper-lined or greased trays and bake at 160°C for 15–20 minutes until lightly browned and slightly firm to the touch. They harden on cooling. (Often these moulds make quite thick biscuits, hence the longer cooking time.) Keep in an airtight container. The flavour will improve after 2–3 days.

**Makes 40 biscuits**

# Cocoa

A pantry without cocoa would be unthinkable for any chocoholic or for anyone with a young family.

Today there are many different brands of cocoa on the market and they are as different as, say, brands of coffee. In fact, like coffee, cocoa beans have to be roasted and husked first. Then different varieties of beans are blended together and ground to make a thick paste (mass) which is then turned into chocolate or cocoa. To make cocoa, cocoa butter is extracted from the paste and the resulting mass is formed into cakes and ground.

There are several varieties of cocoa beans and their flavour is affected by their origin, the roasting process and whether the cocoa has been Dutched. By treating with an alkali to neutralise acidity, Dutching makes cocoa easier to mix in water, it improves the colour and mellows the flavour. Dutch cocoa is best for baking and it can be blended easily for delicious drinks. Most of the cocoa we buy is Dutched, but what makes the difference is the quality of the beans and the cocoa butter content. Experiment with different brands to find the flavour you like best.

## The café chocolate cake

*This dense moist chocolate cake, prepared from cocoa and layered with creamy chocolate butter icing, is sure to become a basic recipe favourite in your home.*

> **175 grams unsalted butter**
> **1 $\frac{1}{2}$ cups caster sugar**
> **2 eggs**
> **2 tblsp golden syrup**
> **1 $\frac{1}{2}$ cups self-raising flour**
> **1 tsp baking soda**
> **$\frac{1}{4}$ cup cocoa**
> **1 $\frac{1}{2}$ cups milk**

### Cook's note

The photo (left) shows two cakes split and joined with a double quantity of chocolate butter icing.

Beat together the butter and sugar until the mixture is very light and creamy and the butter has become very pale.

Add the eggs one at a time and beat well after each addition. Beat in the golden syrup.

In a clean bowl, sift together the flour, baking soda and cocoa and fold into the creamed mixture alternately with the milk.

Turn the mixture into a well-greased, lined 20 cm round cake tin.

Bake at 160°C for 1$\frac{1}{4}$–1$\frac{1}{2}$ hours or until a skewer inserted comes out clean.

Cool in the tin for 10 minutes before turning out onto a cake rack to cool completely. When cold, ice with chocolate butter icing (see recipe below) or decorate with whipped cream.

**Makes 1 cake**

## Chocolate butter icing

> **4 tblsp cocoa**
> **3 tblsp warm milk**
> **100 grams softened butter**
> **1 $\frac{1}{2}$ cups icing sugar, sifted**
> **few drops vanilla essence**

Dissolve the cocoa in the warm milk and allow to cool.

Beat the butter until it is pale and fluffy.

Sift the icing sugar and beat into the creamed butter with the vanilla essence and the cooled cocoa mixture.

# Coconut

Coconut milk, freshly prepared, has a delicate appeal that harmonises exquisitely with many other flavours. The coconut tree is truly indispensable in Polynesia and East Asia. Homes are built from its timber, the coir from the husks is used to weave mats, the leaves make an instant umbrella and the nut itself provides meat and coconut milk.

## Coconut milk or cream?

Coconut cream is thicker and more solid than coconut milk. The cream usually needs to be thinned for use but you can use 1 or 2 tablespoons 'as is' to soften a spicy hot curry. I like the Ayam brand of coconut milk and cream. They also have a 'lite' version, which is handy given coconut's high fat level.

## Coconut crème brûlée

> 2 coconuts
> 2 cups full-cream milk
> about ½–1 cup cream
> 5 egg yolks
> ¼ cup caster sugar
> 1 tsp vanilla essence
> ½ cup caster sugar for topping

Using a screwdriver and hammer, pierce the eyes of the coconuts and turn upside down to drain the liquid (coconut water). Served cold, coconut water is a great thirst quencher.

In a 200°C oven, heat through the coconuts for 10 minutes. Remove from the oven and stand firmly on a bunched tea towel so that they will not move and slip away. Bash the coconuts with the hammer to crack open the nut.

Cut the coconut meat away from the shell. If the meat doesn't come away easily, return the cracked coconut to the oven for a further 5 minutes.

Place the coconut meat in a food processor and process until finely chopped. Pour in the full-cream milk and process to a mulch. If you have time, transfer the mulch to a bowl and refrigerate for 1 hour. Strain through a cloth-lined sieve. Discard the coconut. Measure the coconut-milk mixture and add the cream to make up to 2½ cups.

Beat together the egg yolks, caster sugar, vanilla essence and coconut milk. Strain and pour into six lightly-greased ¾-cup-capacity ramekins. Place in a water bath in the oven and cook at 160°C for 45 minutes. Remove from the oven and leave to stand in the water bath for 15 minutes before transferring to the fridge overnight.

To serve, sprinkle the top liberally with the extra caster sugar. Grill under a very hot grill or use a mini blowtorch to caramelise the caster sugar. Cool for 45 minutes before serving with summer fruit dusted with icing sugar.

**Serves 6**

## Tips and ideas

- Coconuts should be heavy and full of liquid when shaken. If there's no liquid sloshing around inside, it means the coconut is old and rancid.
- There should be no sign of leakage from around the three eyes of the coconut.
- Fresh coconut and coconut milk will go off quickly, even when kept in the refrigerator. If you have excess, freeze the milk. This is best done in ice-cube containers. Once frozen, store the cubes in an airtight bag and use as required.
- Coconut milk and cream will curdle at high temperatures. To prevent this, simmer only and keep the lid off. If the recipe calls for boiling, add a teaspoon of cornflour to the dish — it will help to inhibit the curdling.
- When making your own coconut milk, use 1 cup of milk for every coconut (grated).
- The liquid on the inside of the coconut is called coconut water. It's best used as a drink, served well chilled.

# Coffee

It's fun experimenting with different coffee beans, the size of the grind and the brewing method in search of the perfect coffee to please your taste buds. In world terms, we're late starters in the consumption of gourmet coffee but, in the last two decades, New Zealand's latte society has made up for lost time and meeting friends at the café to enjoy a long black, flat white, espresso or cappuccino is a national pastime. But coffee is good for more than drinking — it's a delicious addition to desserts. Our luscious gateau is a stunning dessert.

## Coffee meringue gateau

1 tsp plunger coffee granules
1 tblsp vanilla essence
6 egg whites
1½ cups caster sugar
½ cup finely chopped toasted hazelnuts

### Filling

2 egg yolks
¼ cup caster sugar
300 gram pouch mascarpone
300 ml cream, thickly whipped
3 tblsp very strong black coffee or coffee liqueur
½ cup chocolate-coated coffee beans
50 grams dark chocolate, melted

Place the coffee granules and vanilla essence in a small bowl. Heat in the microwave on high power for 10 seconds, then strain through a fine sieve. Reserve the liquid.

In a clean bowl beat the egg whites until they form stiff peaks but are not dry. Add the caster sugar 2 tablespoons at a time, beating well after each addition until the mixture is thick and glossy. Gently fold in the hazelnuts and the reserved coffee-vanilla essence.

Line three baking trays with baking paper and mark each with a circle 22 cm in diameter. Divide the mixture among the circles and spread out evenly. Bake at 140°C for 1½ hours or until the meringues are dried out. If possible, swap the trays around in the oven during cooking. Remove the meringues from the oven and allow to cool before peeling away the baking paper. Store in an airtight container.

To prepare the filling, beat the egg yolks and sugar together until thick and creamy. Fold in the mascarpone, whipped cream and coffee or coffee liqueur.

To assemble, sandwich the meringue layers with the coffee cream leaving enough to cover the top lavishly. Decorate with the chocolate-coated coffee beans and a drizzling of melted chocolate. Serve in wedges.

### Cook's note

The meringues and coffee filling can be made in advance and assembled up to three hours before serving. If you wish, add ¼ cup finely chopped toasted hazelnuts to the cream filling.

**Serves 8**

## Tips and ideas

- Contrary to widespread belief, beans or ground coffee should not be kept in a fridge or freezer. Condensation spoils the coffee. Store in a cool, dark place in an airtight container and use within two weeks.
- Keep coffee in an airtight container as it absorbs other aromas.
- Beans should be evenly ground for best results. A burr grinder, rather than a blade grinder, ensures a consistent grind. Wash grinder regularly so no residue remains as this can oxidise between use, causing your next cup to harbour unpleasant flavours.
- Grind beans just before use. The sooner the water comes into contact with the grind, the more likely you are to trap the precious aromatic oils.
- As opposed to tea, coffee should be kept off the boil; boiling water brings out the bitterness in coffee.
- A guide for making coffee using any brewing method is: 1 rounded dessertspoon per person.
- Use strong coffee as a flavouring for cakes, biscuits or desserts.

# Coriander

This pungent herb has exploded into our culinary repertoire following the increased interest in Asian cuisine. Known for its distinctive notes and refreshing qualities, coriander is a must in the kitchen, especially during our sunnier months.

## Storing

Coriander is best bought whole, stem and roots still attached. Wash well to remove any dirt. Place in a plastic bag with a tad of water, blow up with your own breath and seal with a twisty tie. Stand in the fridge, the roots in the water. It will keep this way for a long time. Rinse every second day. If you have leaves, rinse them in cold water, shake and place in a bag blown up with your breath and seal. Keep in the fridge.

## Coriander and coconut chicken salad

### Dressing

1 cup light olive oil
½ cup coriander leaves
1 shallot, peeled
2 tblsp fine white wine vinegar
salt and pepper to season
lime juice

### Salad

440 ml can coconut cream
2 cm piece fresh ginger, sliced
pared rind of 1 lime
1 tblsp chopped coriander root
1 double breast of chicken, skin removed
½ fresh pineapple, peeled and eyes removed
1 mango
4 spring onions, trimmed and sliced
½ cup roughly chopped coriander leaves
¼ cup mint leaves
salad greens for 4, washed and dried

### Garnish

4 poppadums, to serve
toasted peanuts
grated coconut (freshly grated is great)

## Tips and ideas

- Scatter coriander seeds around the garden regularly during the year. It will grow reasonably well all year.
- The leaves look similar to Italian parsley, but give them a rub and a sniff for that distinctive pungent fragrance.
- In Thai cookery the root, stem and leaves are used. The spice is also frequently used in Mexican and North African cookery.
- Coriander goes well with seafood, beef and chicken, and also with the following combinations: mint, basil and parsley; garlic, lemon, chillies, sesame, coconut and ginger; tomatoes, avocados, lettuce and onions; pineapple, mangoes and pawpaw.

Purée the oil, coriander and shallot together in a blender. Stand 1 hour and then strain through a fine sieve. Add the vinegar and season with salt, pepper and lime juice.

Put the coconut cream, ginger, lime rind, coriander root and chicken breast into a saucepan and simmer for 20 minutes until the chicken is cooked. Remove chicken, cool quickly and chill. Discard the coconut cream.

Finely slice the pineapple into rings and cut it into wedges. Cut down the sides of the mango, leaving the large centre stone. Slice each mango half, then turn inside out so that the juicy flesh can be easily removed. Slice the cold chicken breast.

In a bowl toss together the chicken, fruit, spring onions, coriander and mint. Season with salt and pepper. Refrigerate for 30 minutes. Toss chicken through lettuce and drizzle with oil. Serve in a crisp poppadum shell garnished with peanuts and coconut.

**Serves 4**

# Fennel seeds

Everyone who has dined in an Indian restaurant will have been served fennel seeds. Sugar-coated, they're offered after a meal to freshen the breath. But these tender, green, spiky seeds have an amazing flavour when toasted and added to food. Crack a fennel seed between your teeth and allow the warm (but not hot) aniseed taste to tingle your tongue. Fennel is one of the ingredients in Chinese five-spice powder (the others being cassia, star anise, black pepper or Sichuan pepper and cloves). The seeds can be bought from specialty shops in small quantities. Go for the brightest green — a mark of good flavour — and look for the very aromatic Lucknow fennel from India. Store in an airtight container, away from moisture.

## Prawns with Lucknow fennel

*Garlic prawns have always been a favourite, but add slivers of fresh ginger and a good sprinkling of fennel seeds, serve them on slices of sweet cantaloupe melon with warm sautéed leek and fennel bulb and the old favourite takes on a fantastic new guise.*

> 150 grams unsalted butter or ½ cup light olive oil
> 2 tsp Lucknow or best-quality fennel seeds
> 6 cloves garlic, peeled and sliced
> 2 cm piece fresh ginger, finely sliced
> 500 grams green prawns, shelled

### Garnish
> 25 grams butter or 3 tblsp olive oil
> 1 leek, trimmed, washed well and very finely shredded
> 1 fennel bulb, trimmed of the core and very finely shredded
> 2 tblsp chopped, fresh fennel (or 1 tblsp dried fennel)
> ½ cantaloupe melon, deseeded and thinly sliced

Heat the butter or oil in a deep frying pan and add the fennel seeds, garlic and ginger. Cook over a moderate heat for 1 minute until they are fragrant.

Add the prawns and cook them, tossing regularly to coat them in the flavoured butter or oil. Once the prawns turn from green or white to pink, season with salt, set aside and keep warm.

Prepare the garnish. Heat the butter in a frying pan and quickly pan-fry the shredded leek and fennel and, when just wilting, stir in the chopped fennel. Season with salt and pepper.

Arrange a few slices of cantaloupe on plates, top with equal amounts of the leek mix and arrange the prawns on top. Enjoy with crusty bread to mop up the juices.

**Serves 4**

# Filé powder

Filé powder is the ground, dried leaves of the American sassafras tree. It is used in the Creole dishes of Louisiana, specifically gumbos — the big, hearty stews of chicken, smoked pork and/or shellfish. Filé powder has a light spicy flavour, but its main use is as a thickening agent. Boiled in the gumbo, it gives a characteristic stringy texture to the stew. Or if, like us, you'd rather have a smoother, velvety sauce, the filé should be stirred in at the end of cooking. Simply remove the gumbo from the heat before the powder is added. Then, after adjusting the seasoning, the gumbo is served. Try using a tablespoon or so of filé powder to thicken your own soups or stews.

## Chicken and smoked pork gumbo

**1.5 kg corn-fed chicken, cut into 8 portions**
**3 tblsp clarified butter or oil**
**2–3 tblsp flour**
**2 tblsp tomato paste**
**400 gram can tomatoes in juice, chopped**
**3 cups chicken stock**
**2 onions, peeled and chopped**
**2 peppers, deseeded and chopped**
**2–3 stalks celery, sliced**
**2 tsp minced garlic**
**1 large red chilli, deseeded and chopped**
**500 grams sliced smoked pork sausage (such as cabanossi from the supermarket deli)**
**¼–½ tsp cayenne pepper**
**black pepper**
**1 tblsp fresh thyme leaves**
**1 tblsp filé powder**

Brown chicken pieces until golden in 2 tablespoons clarified butter or oil. Drain well. Reserve.

Stir flour into residue butter and cook the roux, stirring continuously, until it turns a caramel colour. Add tomato paste, canned tomatoes and chicken stock, stirring well until the sauce thickens.

In another pan, gently fry onions, peppers and celery in 1 tablespoon clarified butter or oil, thus creating what is known as the Holy Trinity of Louisiana cooking. Add garlic and chilli and continue cooking until the vegetables are tender, but not brown.

Combine the cooked vegetables and sauce. Add the browned chicken and smoked sausage. Season with cayenne, black pepper and thyme. Cover and simmer very gently for about 30–35 minutes or until the chicken is tender and cooked through.

Remove from the heat, stir in filé powder to thicken. Season. Serve immediately with boiled rice. Garnish with fresh thyme.

**Serves 6**

# Fish sauce

Pungent — almost off-putting for some — fish sauce adds that complex and unique flavour which makes many Asian dishes so intriguing and enjoyable. The sauce is prepared from small fish after they are packed with salt in wooden barrels and left to ferment in the sun. The resulting liquid continues to mature in the sun before being bottled.

In Asian cooking, fish sauce frequently acts as a substitute for salt as well as adding vitamin B to diets often lacking in it.

Colour and price are a general guide to quality: darker sauces are of a higher grade and more expensive than lighter sauces. Fish sauce lasts indefinitely in the cupboard but buy it in small quantities so you can experiment with the various brands to find one you like.

## Chicken and crab rolls with Vietnamese dipping sauce

**250 grams minced chicken**
**175 gram can crabmeat, well drained**
**½ cup chopped spring onions**
**60 grams rice vermicelli, soaked and roughly chopped (see Cook's note)**
**1 carrot, peeled and grated**
**2 tblsp each chopped fresh mint, basil and coriander**
**1 tsp minced garlic**
**1 egg**
**1 tblsp cornflour**
**salt and pepper to season**
**1 cup warm water**
**4 tblsp sugar**
**30 rice paper wrappers (about 15 cm round)**

### Cook's note
Rice vermicelli needs to be soaked in boiling hot water for about 3–5 minutes to soften before draining well.

### Vietnamese dipping sauce
**1 tsp minced red chilli**
**grated rind and juice of 1 lime**
**¼ cup fish sauce**
**¼ cup water**
**sugar to taste (about 3 teaspoons)**
**1 tblsp toasted peanuts, ground**

In a bowl mix the minced chicken, crabmeat, spring onions, rice vermicelli, carrot, herbs, garlic, egg and cornflour with a good seasoning of salt and pepper.

In a bowl mix warm water with sugar and stir until dissolved. Place one rice paper wrapper in the warm water at a time and soak for about 30 seconds. Remove and stand until softened.

Place a large tablespoonful of mixture at one edge of the wrapper. Fold over the edges and roll up to enclose. Place on a try lined with baking paper while preparing the others.

Deep-fry 2–3 rolls in hot oil (180°C) for about 3–4 minutes until golden brown. Drain on paper towel and serve hot with the Vietnamese Dipping Sauce made by mixing together all the ingredients. Add sufficient sugar to the sauce to sweeten.

**Makes 30 rolls**

# French tarragon

French tarragon (*Artemisia dracunculus*) is a welcome summer guest that only stays a short while. So be quick to use it in many meals, from salads, seafood and poultry to veal and egg dishes. Two of this herb's quintessential partners are salmon and asparagus, combined here in this summer salad. Don't be fooled by its poor cousin, Russian tarragon. As opposed to the aromatic, slender, green leaves of its French counterpart, Russian tarragon has coarse leaves with little or no flavour and will only disappoint.

## Salmon salad and creamy tarragon dressing

2 cups water
1/4 cup dry white wine
1 bouquet garni
a few peppercorns
800 g–1 kg side of salmon
1 red and 1 yellow pepper
mixed salad greens for 8
1 orange (optional)
8 asparagus spears
2 spring onions, trimmed and chopped

### Tarragon cream dressing

1 egg
2 tblsp caster sugar
3 tblsp tarragon vinegar
1/4 cup cream
1 tblsp finely chopped crystallised ginger (optional)
2 tblsp chopped tarragon

Put the water, wine, bouquet garni and peppercorns in a large lidded frying pan and simmer for 5 minutes. Use tweezers to remove the bones from the salmon and cut into 4 equal-sized pieces. Add the salmon steaks to the pan, cover and poach for 7 minutes or until just cooked. Transfer the salmon to a plate, discarding the liquid. When cool, remove the skin and flake the flesh. Cover and set aside.

Grill the peppers until they are blackened and blistered all over. Cool, peel, core and slice thinly. Refresh the salad greens in cold water and dry well in a salad spinner or wrap in a tea towel and shake lightly. Grate the rind from the orange. Cut away the pith and segment the flesh. Toss together the salmon, asparagus, peppers, lettuce, spring onions, orange rind and segments.

In a heatproof bowl, beat together the egg, sugar and tarragon vinegar. Put the bowl over the top of a saucepan of simmering water and stir constantly until the mixture thickens. Remove from the heat and cool. (Alternatively, microwave on 50 percent power for 30–60 seconds.)

Beat the cream until it just begins to thicken. Fold the cooled egg mixture, ginger and chopped tarragon into the whipped cream.

Spoon the dressing over the salad just before serving.

**Serves 8**

## Tips and ideas

- To make tarragon vinegar, place a bunch of tarragon leaves in a stoppered bottle or jar and cover with wine or cider vinegar. Allow to stand in a warm, sunny place for 3 weeks, shaking daily. Strain and then transfer to a clean bottle. Place a fresh sprig of tarragon into the bottle for decoration, if wished.
- 'Fines herbes' is a classic French herb mixture made from three parts parsley to one part each of tarragon, chervil and chives, all well chopped and blended together. Truly memorable in an omelette!
- Add chopped tarragon or 'fines herbes' to softened butter, roll up in foil or baking paper and refrigerate until firm. Slice and serve on top of barbecued meat or whole baked potatoes during summer.
- Add chopped tarragon to a tub of light sour cream and use as a dip for crudités.

# Garlic

Though the popularity of garlic has see-sawed throughout history, it's very much part of our cuisine again — preferable roasted or served in a variety of dishes. Once roasted, garlic's natural sugars caramelise to add a subtle flavour to your cooking — unlike raw garlic. This garlic soup is one simple way of enjoying garlic's delicate side. And don't worry about bad breath — once cooked, garlic doesn't linger!

## Roasted garlic soup

> **2 bulbs garlic, halved horizontally**
> **oil**
> **4 large onions, peeled**
> **50 grams butter**
> **6 cloves garlic, peeled and crushed**
> **2 tblsp flour**
> **4 cups chicken stock**
> **1 bay leaf**
> **1 tsp red wine vinegar or balsamic vinegar (optional)**
> **salt and freshly ground black pepper to season**

Place the halved garlic bulbs in a roasting dish and drizzle with a little oil. Cover and bake at 180°C for 25 minutes, until a skewer can easily pierce the garlic. Cool.

Slice the onions into thick rings, about 0.5 cm wide.

Heat butter in a large heavy-lidded saucepan then add the onions and cloves of garlic. Cook over a moderate heat until onions are well browned. Add flour; cook 2 minutes.

Gradually stir in the chicken stock until you have a thin, smooth soup. Add bay leaf. Cover and simmer for 10 minutes. Season with vinegar, salt and pepper. Ladle soup into four large bowls; place half a roasted garlic bulb in each. To eat the roast garlic, you may need a fork and a soup spoon.

**Serves 4**

## Tips and ideas

- Squeeze the roasted garilc pulp and mix with a little oil. Keep well refrigerated in an airtight container. Use a tablespoon at a time to flavour sauces, gravies, mayonnaise or vinaigrettes.
- Squeeze the pulp from one whole roasted bulb and mix into a casserole.
- Mashed potatoes with roasted garlic and parsley are delicious!
- Toss together fresh cooked pasta, roasted garlic pulp, diced fresh tomatoes, chopped basil and a splash of olive oil.
- Mix roasted garlic with sour cream to make an instant dip for a nibble.
- Garlic butter tastes nicer when made with roasted garlic pulp and chopped fresh parsley or sage.

# Ginger

This romantic spice has long been associated with the East. The Chinese believe it sends energy to the solar plexus and, if crystallised and eaten as an alternative to sweets, cuts the richness after a fatty meal. The fresh root (called a rhizome) goes particularly well in pork, beef, chicken, duck, fish, prawn or crab dishes. It is also used in pickling and to make ginger beer.

In its powdered form, it is a must in ginger biscuits, brandy snaps and gingerbread. Stem ginger preserved in syrup is perfect in some puddings, especially rhubarb and ice cream. And if you're a fan of sushi, you'll be familiar with pickled ginger. This is made from baby ginger, sliced thinly and cured in vinegar, salt and sugar. It is usually pinky-beige but may be dyed red.

## Ginger Christmas biscuits

> 250 grams butter
> 1 cup caster sugar
> 1/4 cup golden syrup
> 1 tblsp liquid honey
> 70 gram packet flaked almonds
> 1/2 tsp cinnamon
> 3 tsp ground ginger
> 1 tsp baking soda
> 1 tblsp water
> 3 cups flour

### To decorate

> lightly beaten egg white
> extra flaked almonds
> golden cashews

Put the first seven ingredients into a saucepan and stir gently over a moderate heat until the butter has melted. Bring to the boil and then remove from the heat. Dissolve the baking soda in the water and stir into the butter mixture.

Sift the flour into a large bowl and make a well in the centre. Pour in the butter mixture and using a wooden spoon, mix to a stiff dough. Wrap and refrigerate for 2 hours until firm.

Turn the dough out onto a floured board; knead lightly. Roll out to 0.5 cm thick. Cut out Christmas patterns with biscuit cutters. Transfer the biscuits to a baking tray. Decorate if wished. Brush the edges of the biscuits with beaten egg white and decorate with almonds or golden cashews. The egg white acts as glue.

Bake the biscuits at 180°C for 15 minutes until they are nicely browned. Remove from the oven and leave on the tray for a few minutes before transferring to a cake rack to cool. The shapes will crisp as they cool. Store in an airtight container.

**Makes 40 biscuits (depending on the size)**

# Green tea

Japanese green tea has been highly valued since ancient times for its amazing health benefits. Scientists have confirmed that catechin, the tea's bitter component, eliminates toxins caused by bacteria. It can even prevent the bacteria that causes bad breath. Green tea is rich in vitamin E, which works as an antioxidant. It also aids digestion and rejuvenates the body. The Japanese traditionally drink the tea hot, without sugar or milk, usually following a meal. Its refreshing flavour is particularly appealing in this delicious ice cream — a perfect finale to a special dinner.

## Green tea ice cream

> 1 cup full-cream milk
> ¼ cup caster sugar
> 2 tblsp Japanese green tea leaves or 8 green tea teabags
> 4 egg yolks
> 1 cup cream
> 1 tsp freshly squeezed lime juice
> 1–2 drops green food colouring

Heat the milk and sugar until almost boiling. Sprinkle with green tea or add the teabags. Stir and allow to cool. Chill overnight or for at least 2–3 hours or until the milk has sufficient flavour. Strain through a fine sieve.

Heat the milk. Lightly whisk the yolks. Pour the warm milk onto the egg yolks, whisk together and return to the saucepan. Heat gently, stirring continuously until the custard coats the back of a wooden spoon. Do not allow the custard to boil.

Cool, stir in the cream, lime juice and 1–2 drops of green food colouring. Mix well.

Churn in an ice-cream maker, following the manufacturer's instructions, or freeze in a shallow plastic container until slushy, then beat well with a wire whisk. Return to the freezer, then repeat the process after about 3 hours. Freeze until ready to use.

To serve, partially soften in the refrigerator for 30 minutes. Accompany with fresh fruit and garnish with lime rind.

**Serves 4–6**

# Hazelnut oil

Crunching into warm, peeled and freshly roasted hazelnuts is nothing short of heavenly. There's an explosion of sweetness and, of course, that wonderful hazelnut flavour.

Hazelnut oil is a deep russet colour and has an almost overpowering nutty aroma. Expensive to buy, it is often used to dress a salad or maybe a risotto and is delicious over a dessert where hazelnuts themselves are included.

I like to use it in baking — especially in these immensely satisfying biscuits that are perfect to serve with a special coffee for friends in winter (try one flavoured with Frangelico liqueur for a complete hazelnut rush).

Using hazelnut oil also makes these biscuits dairy-free and they are ideal as a replacement for the rather overdone biscotti.

The best hazelnut oil will come with a use-by date and it should be kept well away from heat and light which can turn it rancid. I like the Clovis brand, available from good specialty shops. It is sold in a metal tin, perfect for storage.

## Hazelnut biscuits

> 1 cup hazelnut oil (see Cook's note)
> ¾ cup sugar
> 1 egg
> 2 cups flour
> 1 tsp baking powder
> ¼ cup finely chopped, toasted hazelnuts
> about 15 hazelnuts, halved

In a bowl, mix together the hazelnut oil, sugar and egg.

Sift together the flour and baking powder and stir into the bowl with the finely chopped hazelnuts.

Roll heaped teaspoonfuls of mixture into balls and place on a greased baking tray. Place a halved hazelnut into the centre of each biscuit.

Bake at 160°C for 15–20 minutes until lightly golden. Cool on a cake rack and then store in an airtight container.

**Makes 30 biscuits**

### Cook's note
For a more economical recipe, use half hazelnut oil with half canola oil.

# Juniper berries

Crunch a few dried, yet juicy, juniper berries and the aroma of gin will hit you. From the Dutch word 'jenever', the ebony and purple fruit gave the alcoholic spirit its name. Juniper berries bring freshness to cooking; they cut the gaminess of meat dishes such as venison and the fat in dishes such as duck. Try a squashed berry or two in a favourite red wine marinade for steak, add one or two to a traditional turkey stuffing or scatter a few in a roasting pan with vegetables for pork or chicken. Buy them from a delicatessen and store in an airtight container away from heat and light.

## Chicken with juniper

*This rich, red-wine-based chicken casserole is scented gently with juniper berries. Crush them just before using so their flavour won't be lost.*

> 1.5 kg chicken or 8 chicken pieces
> 750 ml bottle good Merlot or Pinot Noir
> 3 onions, peeled and quartered
> 4 stalks celery, cut into chunks
> 8–10 cloves garlic, crushed but with their skins left on
> 1 small handful fresh thyme
> 1 small handful fresh oregano
> 2 bay leaves
> 12 juniper berries, crushed
> 1 tsp each cracked pepper and salt
> ¼ cup oil (olive is good here)
> 6 tblsp tomato paste

Joint the chicken, if whole, into 8 pieces and place them into a large dish in one layer. Pour over the wine and scatter over the onion, celery, garlic, thyme, oregano, bay leaves, juniper berries, pepper and salt. Cover and refrigerate overnight.

Heat the oil in a large flameproof casserole. Strain the wine from the chicken and reserve. Brown the chicken pieces well and set aside. Add the vegetables to the pan and brown in the hot oil. Add the tomato paste and cook until it turns from bright red to a deep brown-red colour.

Pour in the reserved wine and bring to the boil. Return the chicken pieces to the casserole and cover.

Cook in a 160°C oven for 1 hour or until the chicken is tender.

Alternatively, simmer very gently on top of the stove for an hour, stirring occasionally. Serve on polenta.

Variation: add 2 sliced pears or apples at step 3, if wished.

**Serves 4–6**

# Kaffir lime leaves

Intensely fragrant, 'double-jointed' kaffir lime leaves add unrivalled flavour to Asian cuisine. For the first time in New Zealand we are able to buy the plants and grow them in warmer climes or we can purchase the emerald-green leaves fresh or dried from specialty Asian food stores. Kaffir lime leaves (also known as makrut leaves) are well worth hunting for. However, if you cannot find them near you, use a tender young leaf from a lime or lemon tree.

## Spicy salmon and prawn fish cakes

500 grams boneless salmon
250 grams shelled green prawns
4 double-jointed kaffir lime leaves
¼ cup finely chopped shallots or onion
1 tsp minced fresh garlic
1 tsp minced fresh ginger
1–2 tsp finely diced fresh chilli or chilli paste
1 tsp finely sliced lemon grass (optional)
1 tsp ground laos (optional) (see Cook's note)
2 tsp toasted coriander seeds
1 tsp toasted cumin seeds
1 egg white
1 tsp salt
2 tblsp chopped fresh coriander
clarified butter or oil to pan-fry

Cut the salmon into 3 cm pieces and place in a bowl with the prawns. Finely shred the kaffir lime leaves and add them to the bowl with the shallots, garlic, ginger, chilli, lemon grass or laos if using, coriander seeds and cumin seeds. Toss to mix. Cover and marinate salmon and prawns for 15 minutes.

Transfer the ingredients to a food processor and add the egg white, salt and coriander and pulse until the mixture is well chopped but has not become a paste.

Mould large tablespoonfuls of mixture into about 20 even-sized patties.

Heat sufficient butter or oil to just cover the base of a non-stick frying pan and cook the patties for about 5–6 minutes, turning once until they are golden and cooked but not over-cooked.

Serve with chilli dipping sauce to which one or two sliced kaffir lime leaves have been added.

**Makes about 20 patties, to serve 6**

## Cook's note
Laos is a member of the ginger family and the ground powder can be purchased in the spice section of specialty stores. If you do not have any, omit it or add ½ teaspoon ground ginger.

## Tips and ideas
- Add them to a hot bath and they will impart a wonderful fragrance.
- Make an Asian-style bouquet garni to flavour fish, chicken or beef stock as the basis of an Asian-style soup. Use kaffir lime leaves, lemon grass and ginger, omitting the traditional bay leaf bouquet garni.
- Rub the leaf over your hands to freshen them after a long day.
- Add a couple of leaves to the water for cooking jasmine rice.
- Add a leaf to sugar overnight to make sensational lemon cake or add it to a syrup to pour over a cake.
- Flavour a rice pudding with a leaf or two.
- Add a crushed leaf or two to a honey and soy marinade for lamb, chicken or pork.
- If you are a fan of Thai foods, then having these on hand is a must.

# Kelp pepper

Next time you're looking for a healthy new condiment, consider kelp pepper. It comes as dark-green flakes and is actually more salty than peppery. Despite its distinctive sea aroma, kelp pepper is not overpoweringly flavoured when used in small amounts and so it works well with many dishes — especially seafood — where you would normally add salt or where you want extra nutrients. It is rich in iodine and B-group vitamins. Made in the South Island from giant kelp, it is dried, then ground. Kelp pepper easily absorbs liquids so store it somewhere dry and use the coarser grade for cooking. It has been available nationwide for the past few months but received its own glittering debut at the Versace exhibition at Te Papa in 2001 when chef Peter Thornley served thinly sliced tuna rolled in kelp pepper. Bellissimo!

## Southern seas sauce on linguine

**about 1.5 kg green-lipped mussels in shells**
**about 750 grams clams in shells**
**1 cup dry white wine**
**200 grams green prawns, shelled**
**50 grams butter**
**1 onion, peeled and finely chopped**
**1 tsp minced garlic**
**1 red pepper, sliced (optional)**
**2 tblsp flour**
**1/2 cup cream**
**1–2 tsp kelp pepper**
**500 grams linguine pasta**

Discard any mussels or clams that are open. Scrub mussels well and remove their beards. Rinse clams thoroughly under cold running water to remove any excess sand.

Put mussels, clams and wine in a large saucepan, cover and cook over a high heat for about 5 minutes or until the shells have opened.

Drain and reserve the cooking liquid. Discard any mussels or clams that have not opened. Reserve a few mussels in their shells for garnish. Then carefully remove the remaining cooked mussels and clams from their shells. Boil the reserved cooking liquid until it has reduced to about 1 cup.

Gently pan-fry prawns in the butter until they have turned pink. Set aside.

Add the onion, garlic and pepper to the pan and cook gently until the onion has softened. Stir in the flour and cook for 1 minute.

Stir in the reserved cooking liquid and cook until the sauce has thickened. Simmer for 1 minute. Return the prawns to the pan with the mussels and clams, and stir in the cream. Heat through, then season with the kelp pepper and toss through the hot linguine pasta. If wished, garnish with a few mussels in half-shells and a sprinkling of kelp pepper.

**Serves 4–5**

# Lavender

Lavender has been used throughout history and frequently appears in folklore and fairytales. It is said that when Mary placed the infant Jesus' clothes out to dry, she spread them upon a lavender bush and in doing so gave lavender its heavenly perfume. It may also explain why lavender is referred to as 'Our Lady's candlestick'. But lavender has been used for more than scent alone. Napoleon liked a drink made with sugar, musk and chocolate scented with lavender — it was said to be appealing to Josephine. Elizabeth I delighted in lavender conserve and in Provence, France, lavender is still a favoured herb in cooking today. Its culinary uses are wide and varied, adding both comfort and intrigue to sweet and savoury dishes.

## Lavender and orange-infused pears

**4 firm pears that are not too under-ripe (ripe pears take less**
**time to cook)**
**1 cup sugar**
**grated rind of 2 oranges**
**1 cup orange juice**
**about 10 lavender heads**
**2 cups water**
**borage flowers to garnish**

Peel the pears and cut a small piece from the base so that the pears stand upright.

Place the sugar, orange rind and juice, lavender heads and water in a saucepan and bring to the boil. Simmer for 5 minutes, stirring until the sugar dissolves.

Stand the pears upright in the saucepan and cover. Simmer gently for about 30–40 minutes until a skewer inserted can easily be removed. Alternatively, bake at 180°C for about 50 minutes.

Transfer the pears to a plate. Remove the lavender heads and simmer the syrup until reduced by one-third. Stand the pears in a serving dish and pour over the warm syrup. Garnish with borage flowers. Serve hot or cold.

**Serves 4**

## Tips and ideas

- Don't over-boil lavender as it will make its camphor-like undertones come through.
- Infuse sugar with lavender heads instead of vanilla.
- Infuse lavender heads in hot tea, strain and use as a base for punch.
- Simmer raspberries or strawberries with lavender before removing and turning the fruit into jam.
- Infuse milk and/or cream with lavender and use to make lavender ice cream, lavender creamed rice or lavender baked custard.
- Hang bunches of lavender scented with a little lavender oil and tied with large rustic ribbons around your house. The scent will relax you.
- Tie a bunch of lavender heads in a muslin bag and hang it under running bath water for a fabulous scented bath.

# Lemon balm

Bees love lemon balm (*Melissa officinalis*) so much so that it is also known as 'bee balm'. However, the highly-scented leaves from this wonderful perennial herb are ideal to grow in the garden, not only to encourage the bees, but also to add charm to your summer cooking. Gather handfuls of the leaves of this hardy, easy-care plant and use them to scent this delicious jelly, perfect for savouring with friends or family after a lazy lunch.

## Lemon balm jelly

> 1 firmly packed cup lemon balm leaves, washed
> 2 ½ cups fruity Riesling
> 4 tblsp brandy
> rind of 1 lemon
> 1 cup water
> ½ cup sugar
> 5 tsp gelatin
> green food colouring (optional)

Place the lemon balm, Riesling, brandy, lemon rind, half the water and the sugar in a bowl and stir to dissolve the sugar. Using a spoon or wooden spoon, press the leaves against the side of the bowl to release their oils. Stand for 30 minutes, then strain.

Sprinkle the gelatin over the remaining water and stand 10 minutes to sponge. Dissolve by standing over hot water or by placing in the microwave for 10 seconds on high. Stir to dissolve.

Place the strained lemon balm and wine mixture into a saucepan and colour with green food colouring if wished. Bring to a medium heat, but do not boil. Add the dissolved gelatin and stir over a low heat for 1–2 minutes to dissolve thoroughly.

Pour into four 1 cup- or two 2 cup-capacity jelly moulds. Cool, then refrigerate for four hours or until set.

Serve with fresh fruit such as diced pineapple scented with sliced lemon balm.

**Serves 4**

## Tips and ideas

- Slice leaves and add to fresh fruit salads.
- Place leaves in a posy on the bedside table as it is said to be mildly sedative.
- Soak plenty of crushed leaves in a light olive oil to make lemon balm oil. Great to toss through a salad or over prawns from the barbecue.
- Chicken stuffing seasoned with balm is a sheer taste sensation.
- Add a leaf or two to a teapot with your normal teabag or leaves for a deliciously refreshing brew.
- Slice and toss with steamed summer vegetables such as asparagus, mangetouts and beans.
- The leaves are great in punches. Don't forget to crush them first to release their oils.

# Lemon thyme

Lemon thyme is a cross between garden and wild thyme. Its bright green leaves have a sensational lemon tang and it is so wonderfully tantalising in summer. Its sweet citrus notes make it a perfect partner to chicken, seafood, pasta and vegetable dishes.

## Lemon thyme roasted poussins

4 poussins
100 grams butter, softened
3 tblsp chopped lemon thyme
2 tsp ground black pepper
2 tblsp honey (a mild-flavoured honey is best here)
2 lemons

Wash the poussins under running cold water and pat dry on absorbent paper. Cut off and discard the neck if still attached.

Mix the butter, lemon thyme, pepper and honey together to form a smooth paste. Using your thumbs, carefully lift the skin away from the breast.

Spread out 1 tablespoonful of the herb butter mixture under the skin of each poussin.

Spread the remaining herb butter mixture evenly over the poussins. Tie the poussins in shape with string and place on a foil-lined baking tray. Cut the lemons in half and place the 4 halves cut-side down on the foil beside the poussins.

Bake at 190°C for 40–45 minutes until the poussins are golden and cooked. To test if the meat is done, pierce the thigh joint of the poussins with a skewer. If the juices are clear the birds are done. If they are still pink, cook a little longer.

Serve with the roasted lemons, which can be squeezed over the poussins. Add a summer salad of greens to accompany.

**Serves 4**

## Tips and ideas

- While it grows easily in most New Zealand gardens, lemon thyme is available pre-packaged in your supermarket vegetable department.
- It is best partnered with seafood and chicken, although it is also delicious sprinkled over barbecued courgettes, mangetout or green beans.
- Tie bundles of lemon thyme onto pork sausages before cooking and glaze with honey before serving.
- Finely chop the leaves and add them to a peach or apricot compote or a fresh fruit jelly.
- Mix chopped lemon thyme leaves into sweetened whipped cream or mascarpone and serve with poached fruits in summer.
- In winter, if you are a creamed rice fan, add a few sprigs to the rice and milk while cooking.
- When poaching chicken, add a few sprigs to the water.
- Beyond cooking: add a handful of lemon thyme to a bubble bath — the scent is wonderful and the bath even more relaxing.

# Lime

No other citrus fruit has quite the tang of limes. A drink of lime juice and soda with a slice of fresh lime is one of summer's best thirst quenchers, while toast thickly spread with lime honey leaps into another dimension. Limes were valued by English sailors in centuries past as a preventative for scurvy. This led to the famous sobriquet 'Limeys'.

Vivid green limes add panache to a fruit bowl and their crisp, clean tang brings many foods to life. My favourite ways with limes are often the simplest, like this lime honey — simple to make and ideal to bottle as a gift.

## Lime honey

**4 large eggs**
**pinch salt**
**125 grams unsalted butter, melted**
**1 cup sugar**
**grated rind and juice of 4 large or 6 small limes**

Beat the eggs with a pinch of salt until smooth. Strain.

Place the eggs, melted butter, sugar, lime rind and juice into the top of a double saucepan.

Cook over simmering water for about 10–15 minutes, stirring constantly until thickened.

Put into hot sterilised jars and cover until cool. Seal and label.

**Makes 3 cups**

## Tips and ideas

- Make quick mini tarts by filling pre-baked mini sweet pastry tarts with lime honey. Serve with coffee.
- Whip $1/2$ cup cream until thick and fold into 1 cup cold lime honey. Use to top a meringue or a sponge roll, as a trifle filling or for tiramisu with a difference.
- Label bottles of lime honey and use as gifts for friends.
- Take two sheets of pre-rolled puff pastry, cut in half and bake. Layer with fresh fruit like strawberries or raspberries, whipped cream and lime honey. Dust with icing sugar.
- Serve with fruit or bran muffins in place of butter.

# Manuka honey

No other culinary product offers more variety than honey. Manuka, our most prized, is unique. Its warm, not-too-sweet mellow flavour makes it highly regarded world-wide and it is considered a connoisseur's honey, a perfect partner for many foods.

There are subtle differences between manuka honey from the North and South Islands but these just add to its mystical charm. Partnering manuka honey with manuka-smoked lamb creates a sensational Kiwi dish.

## Manuka-smoked rack of lamb with macadamia nut crumb

### Lamb

2 racks lamb, trimmed (each with 8 cutlets)
about 1½–2 cups manuka wood shavings (from the hardware store)
1½ cups fresh white breadcrumbs
¾ cup macadamia nuts, roughly chopped
75 grams butter, chilled
2 tblsp manuka honey
1 tblsp chopped fresh marjoram

### Manuka honey jus

2 cups mild-flavoured beef stock
1 cup Pinot Noir
¼ cup port
1 small bouquet garni
2 tblsp manuka honey
cornflour to thicken
salt and pepper to season
about 25 grams butter

Place the lamb on a roasting rack.

Scatter the manuka shavings over the base of an oven tray and place near the bottom of a 200°C oven. Allow the shavings to smoke, then turn the oven to 120°C and place the lamb at the top of the oven and smoke for 8 minutes. Quickly remove — beware of any smoke alarms! Cool the lamb, cover and refrigerate until required. Allow the manuka shavings to stop smoking and to cool completely before discarding.

In a food processor, put the breadcrumbs, macadamia nuts, butter, honey and marjoram and process until all ingredients are finely chopped. Press equal amounts of the mixture firmly onto the meaty part of the lamb racks.

Bake at 200°C for 25–30 minutes. Stand 5 minutes before carving. Serve with the manuka honey jus, sautéed diced pumpkin and green vegetables.

**Serves 4–5**

### Honey jus

Place the beef stock, wine, port, bouquet garni and honey into a saucepan and simmer gently until reduced to 1–1¼ cups. Remove the bouquet garni.

Mix about 2–3 teaspoons cornflour with a good dash of port and use to thicken the jus to your liking. Season with salt and pepper and, just before serving, whisk in the butter.

**Makes 1–1¼ cups**

## Tips and ideas

- Use one-third manuka honey with one-third cider vinegar and one-third olive oil to make a fabulous salad dressing.
- If you make your own bread, try adding a spoonful of manuka honey. It will offer a subtle underlying flavour and give the loaf a warm, finished colour as well as helping the bread keep longer.
- Try blue brie with manuka honey — it's delicious.
- A splash of manuka honey in a chicken or lamb tagine (a Middle Eastern stew) will add a magic sweetness to the sauce.
- Honey burns quickly when in contact with direct heat (on a barbecue) or prolonged heat (basting a roast) so use sparingly in marinades and glazes. Brush it on closer to the end of cooking for final colour and flavour.
- Be bold, try different honeys. We have some of the finest in the world.

# Mascarpone

Velvety and luxurious, mascarpone has become the queen of the cream world. Often referred to as mascarpone cheese, it is actually a cream — and a very rich one at that.

Kapiti Cheese makes most of the mascarpone in New Zealand. A culture is added to rich local cream before it is heated and allowed to mature and thicken. With a fat content of 37 percent, it adds richness to many dishes and is wonderfully versatile, although I serve it as simply as I can to enjoy its smooth, rich taste and texture.

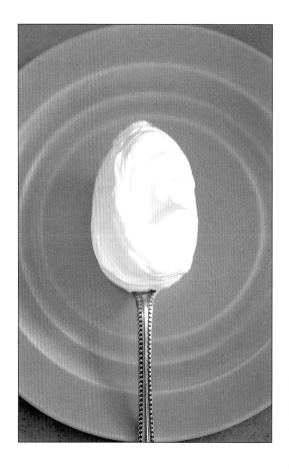

## Quick mascarpone fruit tarts

### Pastry
**2 cups flour**
**¼ cup sugar**
**150 grams butter**
**3–4 tblsp cold water**

### Filling
**1½ cups mascarpone**
**1 tblsp sugar**
**2 egg yolks**
**2 cups berries (fresh, or frozen and defrosted)**
**¼ cup brown sugar**

Make the pastry. In a food processor, process flour, sugar and butter together until the mixture looks like crumbs. Pulse in sufficient water to make small, moist balls of dough. Turn out and bring together on a floured board. Divide the dough into 6 portions and roll each out large enough to line the base and sides of 6 x 12 cm tartlet tins. Cover the pastry with baking paper and weight with beans. Bake blind at 200°C for 15 minutes. Remove paper and beans. Return to the oven for a further 3–4 minutes, until the pastry is well cooked.

Mix together the mascarpone, sugar and egg yolks until smooth.

Sprinkle enough berries into each tartlet to just cover the base. Spread a thick layer of the mascarpone mixture on top. Wrap pastry edges in foil to prevent them from burning. Sprinkle with a thick layer of brown sugar and place under a hot grill for 1–2 minutes, until the mascarpone has melted and started to brown.

Variation: use two cans of well-drained tropical fruit chunks for an exotic summery taste.

**Makes 6 x 12 cm tarts**

## Tips and ideas
- Serve it alongside your favourite tart, especially ones that have a sharpness to them, such as lemon tart.
- Spread it on toasted fruit bread, bagels or a warm croissant with jam or marmalade.
- Splash out and make a tiramisu.
- Add grated lemon or lime rind to mascarpone and sweeten with icing sugar. Serve with tropical fruit.
- Use in a baked cheesecake for a delicious melt-in-your-mouth texture.
- In summer, serve it with icing sugar-dusted berries and shortbread thins for a simple and elegant dessert.
- If you are making a special cheese tart or flan, use mascarpone for a smoother texture.

# Miso

Miso is a delicious, highly nutritious seasoning which has been an integral part of the Japanese diet and culture for centuries. All miso is made by mixing cooked soy beans with rice, wheat or barley or a combination of these. A yeast-like culture and sea salt are added and then the miso is left to mature, under pressure, for anything from a few months to many years.

Miso is sold in a variety of types but the most common one in New Zealand is Marukura organic white. This has a slightly sweet, caramelised flavour with a creamy texture. The darkest of all miso — organic unpasteurised Hatcho — is very dense with a rich fragrance and full-bodied taste.

Miso's sweet and salty characteristics make it incredibly versatile. It can be used to enhance the taste of vegetables, seafood, tofu and meat or to add flavour to soups and casseroles. Mix miso with oil and vinegar and use as a dressing or brush it as a paste over roasted vegetables and meat. Stored in the refrigerator, it will keep for months. Miso is readily available from good health-food stores, Asian food stores and the deli department of some supermarkets.

## Roast winter vegetables with miso

about 500 grams each kumara, pumpkin, carrots and parsnips, peeled
    and cut into even-sized pieces
1–2 tblsp sesame oil
2–3 leeks, trimmed, halved lengthways and cut into 7–8 cm lengths

### White miso paste
4 tblsp white miso
1½ tblsp palm sugar, grated
1 tblsp sherry or mirin (sweet Japanese rice wine)
1 tblsp fresh lime or lemon juice
1 tsp fresh lime or lemon rind
1 tblsp coriander, freshly chopped

### Brown miso paste
2 tblsp brown Hatcho miso
1½ tblsp palm sugar, grated
2 tblsp sherry
1 tblsp minced fresh ginger
1 red chilli, deseeded and finely chopped

Place prepared kumara, pumpkin, carrots and parsnips in a plastic bag. Add sesame oil. Toss to coat. Arrange in a single layer on a lined oven tray and cook at 190°C for about 25 minutes or until vegetables are barely tender. Reduce oven to 180°C.

Combine white miso with palm sugar, sherry and lime juice until smooth. Stir in lime rind and coriander.

In a separate bowl, mix brown miso with palm sugar and sherry until smooth. Add ginger and chilli, mix well to combine.

Brush half the roasted vegetables and half the leeks with the white miso. Brush remainder with brown miso paste. Return to oven. Cook for an extra 15–20 minutes or until vegetables are golden and tender.

**Serves 6**

# Oregano

Oregano has a robust, spicy flavour, which makes it a perfect match for tomato-based sauces, aubergine, seafood and grilled meats. The perennial herb originated in ancient Greece and its name means 'Joy of the Mountain' because the attractive fragrant plant was once found growing on hilltops. While synonymous with Italian and Greek cuisine (who could imagine moussaka without oregano?), the herb's aromatic flavour can also enhance the hotter, spicier foods of North Africa and Mexico. Oregano is closely related to marjoram but is slightly more pungent. Use it fresh or dried.

## Italian meatloaf

*Oregano turns humble meatloaf into an exciting Italian experience. Don't be tempted to add milk or butter to the potato when you mash it. It doesn't need it — the potato will absorb all the cooking juices from the meatloaf instead. Delicious!*

**800 grams starchy potatoes**
**1 onion, peeled and chopped**
**1 tblsp oil**
**1 red pepper, deseeded and diced**
**750 grams minced pork**
**2 tblsp freshly chopped oregano**
**150 grams mozzarella cheese, grated**

Peel the potatoes and cook in boiling, salted water until tender. Drain and then mash until smooth. Measure 2$\frac{1}{2}$ cups and reserve.

Fry the onion and pepper in oil until tender, but not brown.

In a bowl, combine the cooked onion and red pepper, minced pork and 1 tablespoon chopped oregano. Mix well and season with salt and pepper.

Line the base and sides of a 14 cm x 24 cm loaf tin with foil. Use two-thirds of the pork mixture to cover the base and sides of the prepared tin.

Spread 1$\frac{1}{2}$ cups of mashed potato evenly over the mince mixture. Cover with the mozzarella and sprinkle with the remaining oregano.

Place the remaining mashed potato over the cheese layer, top the potatoes with the remaining pork mince, and press down firmly.

Cook at 180°C for about 45 minutes, or until cooked through and the potato is very hot.

Turn the meatloaf out onto a serving dish and serve sliced, accompanied by a salad or steamed vegetables.

**Serves 4–6**

# Palm sugar

Deep brown or honey-hued, palm sugar is made from the sap of palm trees. It can take up to 15 years for a palm tree to start flowering, and then the sap can be collected.

In Bali, the sap usually comes from coconut palms. Tapped from young stalks, it is collected in hollowed coconut shells and then boiled and stirred until it forms a fudge-like mass. Then it is poured into coconut shells, fitted with a piece of palm or banana leaf as decoration. After about 10 minutes the sugar is turned out, packed in woven flax boxes and sold at the village markets. The sugar needs to be grated or crumbled when used and should be kept in an airtight container.

Palm sugar can be made from coconut palms, kitul palms, sugar palms of India and Java, as well as palmyra palms and each has its own flavour. Palm sugar also has many names — *jaggery* or *gur* in India or Sri Lanka (which, confusingly, can also refer to raw cane sugar), *gula melaka* in Malaysia, *gula jawa* in Indonesia and *nam taan peep* in Thailand.

## Palm sugar and lime banana loaf

½ cup grated palm sugar
¼ cup sugar
150 grams butter
2 eggs
grated rind of 2 limes or lemons
1 cup mashed banana (about 3)
2¼ cups self-raising flour
4 tblsp milk
¼ cup pecans or walnuts (optional)

### Lime glaze
1 cup icing sugar
2–3 tblsp lime juice

Beat the palm sugar, sugar and butter together until soft and light. Beat in the eggs and lime rind.

Fold in the banana, sifted flour and the milk.

Turn the dough into a greased and lined 20 cm x 10 cm loaf tin and top with pecans or walnuts, if using.

Bake at 180°C for 45–50 minutes until cooked. Turn onto a cake rack and cover with the lime glaze. Serve sliced warm or cooled.

**Makes 1 loaf**

## Lime glaze
Sift the icing sugar. Mix in the lime juice. Decorate if liked with grated lime rind.

# Pecans

Native to North America, pecan nuts are famous world-wide for their delicious contribution to the dessert trolley — in the form of Pecan Nut Pie. This version is very rich and the cocoa adds a warm mellow flavour. Pecan Pie is best eaten with lashings of whipped cream.

## Pecan and chocolate pie

### Pastry
> 1¼ cups flour
> pinch salt
> ¼ cup caster sugar
> 125 grams butter
> 1–2 tblsp water

### Filling
> about 1½ cups whole pecans
> ¼ cup cocoa
> 6 egg yolks
> ½ cup firmly packed brown sugar
> ½ cup golden syrup
> 75 grams butter
> ¼ cup double cream
> 2 tsp vanilla essence

In a food processor, blend together the flour, salt, sugar and butter until the mixture forms crumbs. Add sufficient water to form small moist balls of dough that will hold together when squeezed in your hand. Turn mixture out, bring together and stand 5 minutes.

Roll out the dough and line the base and sides of a 23 cm loose-bottomed flan tin. Line the inside of the dough with baking paper and fill with blind-baking material (rice, beans, etc). Bake blind at 200°C for 15 minutes then remove the blind-baking material and paper. Place the flan back in the oven for a further 5–8 minutes until cooked.

### Filling
Arrange the pecans evenly over the bottom of the flan, either at random or in a pattern.

In a saucepan put the cocoa, egg yolks, brown sugar, golden syrup, butter, double cream and vanilla essence. Stir over a low heat until the mixture is well blended. Strain through a fine sieve.

Pour slowly over the pecans so that they rise evenly to the top. Bake at 170°C for 40–45 minutes. Stand for 1 hour before serving. Decorate with a dusting of icing sugar and a drizzling of melted dark chocolate if wished.

**Makes 1 pie**

### Cook's note
For a nice change to the pastry, replace the 125 grams butter with 100 grams butter and 50 grams cream cheese.

## Tips and ideas
- Keep this pie covered at room temperature. In the refrigerator it will become hard and chewy.
- Keep pecans (and all other nuts) securely sealed in the freezer. Their high oil content will make them go rancid if left in a hot kitchen cupboard.
- Pecans have more flavour if lightly toasted. Place them in a 180°C oven for 10 minutes. Cool before using.
- Salted pecans are delicious. Toast them as above and while hot toss them in a dash of olive oil and crushed sea salt. Cool.
- Walnuts can be substituted for pecans in all recipes.

# Peppercorns

Pepper accounts for one-quarter of the world's trade in spices. Extensively cultivated throughout the tropics, the pretty climber (*Piper nigrum*) winds its way up tall straight trees. Its thick-vein pointed leaves shade tender clusters of baby peppercorns that hang in bunches, turning from green to yellow to a reddish-pink when fully ripe.

**Black peppercorns** are berries that were picked as they turned red but before they were completely ripe. Dried in the sun, they turn black. When ground, black pepper should look grey. An all-black colour — considered second grade — is produced from berries that are empty or without their heart (white pepper). **Green peppercorns** are unripe berries and they have a subtle flavour. They are too soft for peppermills, so it is best to chop them roughly or use whole. **White peppercorns** are the heart of the berry with its outer skin removed. This process is very time-consuming — hence white pepper's more expensive price. **Pink peppercorns** are soft, fully ripe fruit with a sweet, delicate flavour. They are sold pickled in brine.

## Peppered stir-fry steak and mushrooms

*By sifting ground black pepper to separate the white from the black, you can create a magnificent pepper steak by using just the black pepper. Try this with rump steak, remembering to let it rest before serving — that way the meat will be juicier and very tender.*

 3 tblsp black peppercorns
 500 grams thick-cut rump steak
 ¼ cup port or brandy
 2–3 tblsp olive oil
 2 onions, peeled and finely sliced
 4 large flat mushrooms
 300 ml cream
 1 tsp each mild mustard and salt
 potatoes for 4, prepared your favourite way (mashed, rösti, pan-fried)
 greens for 4

Grind the black pepper (medium setting on the peppermill) and then sieve. Reserve the fine, white pepper and use elsewhere. Cut the rump steak into thick, finger-sized pieces. Dip meat into the port or brandy and sprinkle over the pepper. Stand for 30 minutes.

Heat half the oil in a pan and pan-fry the onions and mushrooms until they are well browned, cooked and fragrant. Keep warm.

Heat the remaining oil in a frying pan or wok and quickly stir-fry the meat until well browned on the outside but still pink inside. Set the meat aside to rest for 2–3 minutes. Add the cream, mustard and salt to the pan and boil for 1–2 minutes, scraping to lift the sediment from the pan.

To serve, arrange your favourite potatoes and greens on a plate, top with mushrooms, onion slices and beef, and then pour over the cream sauce. Serve immediately.

**Serves 4**

# Pistachios

Pistachio nuts have beautiful green kernels with a delicately sweet taste and hard shells that split open when the fruit is ripe. The greener the colour the better the flavour.

They are predominantly grown in Iran, Turkey and California, along with other Mediterranean and Asian countries. The trees live for centuries (one tree in Iran is believed to be 700 years old) and need little or no care.

Americans love them most, consuming a whopping 98 percent of the world supply. Roasted, salted pistachios are perfect with drinks and the nut is used often in both Indian and Mediterranean cooking.

Italian mortadella sausage is usually studded with pistachios. And you'll find the nut in other favourites such as baklava, Turkish delight, stuffings for meat and fish, Persian rice and pistachio ice cream — not, of course, forgetting pistachio biscotti.

## Pistachio biscotti

> 2¾ cups flour
> 1 tsp baking powder
> ½ tsp baking soda
> ½ tsp salt
> 125 grams unsalted butter
> 1 cup caster sugar
> 3 eggs
> 1 tsp finely grated lemon rind
> 1 tblsp mixed peel (optional)
> ¼ cup dried apricot pieces
> 2 x 70 gram packets (about 1 cup) shelled and unsalted pistachio nuts

Sift together the flour, baking powder, baking soda and salt.

Beat the butter and sugar together until the mixture is light and fluffy. Add the eggs one at a time, beating well after each addition.

Beat in the rind, peel and apricots.

Stir in the flour mixture and pistachios. Turn onto a lightly floured surface. Knead for 1 minute.

Shape into sausage-like rolls, about 3 cm in diameter and the length of your baking tray. Flatten the sausage shapes a little.

Bake at 160°C for 30 minutes, then allow the logs to cool on the tray for 10 minutes. Cut the logs on the diagonal into slices 0.5–1 cm thick.

Place the biscotti on the tray and return to the oven for 5 minutes. Turn them over and cook for a further 5 minutes. Cool on a wire rack and store in an airtight container.

**Makes 40 biscotti**

# Pomegranate

According to Arab mythology, the apples in the Garden of Eden were actually pomegranates. They're quite the designer fruit — bulbous and irregular, ranging in shades from lemon to soft pink to crimson. Inside the tough outer skin is a mass of bitter seeds held in tiny sacks of sweet rose-red pulp. The crunchy seeds add life to casseroles while concentrated pomegranate juice casts a magical spell over simple dishes, making it near impossible for guests to guess the secret ingredient. Pomegranates aren't common here, although you may see them in autumn or imported in spring, but you can use their unusual-tasting juice all year round.

## Rack of lamb with shallot and pomegranate marmalade

2 tsp concentrated pomegranate juice
1 tsp grated fresh ginger
1 tsp sherry
pepper
2 lamb racks, trimmed

### Shallot and pomegranate marmalade

750 grams shallots, peeled
¼ cup olive oil
grated rind and juice of 2 oranges
½ cup sugar
2–4 tblsp concentrated pomegranate juice
salt and pepper to taste

Mix together the concentrated pomegranate juice, grated ginger and sherry and a good seasoning of pepper. Score the back of the lamb racks diagonally in a criss-cross fashion. Rub the pomegranate marinade into the lamb. Cover and set aside in the refrigerator to marinate for 1 hour or overnight.

To prepare the marmalade, cut the shallots into thick wedge-like slices. Heat the olive oil in a large frying pan and fry shallot wedges over a moderate heat for about 15–20 minutes until they are very soft.

Add the orange rind and juice, the sugar and the second measure of concentrated pomegranate juice. Season to taste. Simmer gently for about 10 minutes until the mixture is thick and marmalade-like. Place in an airtight container and keep covered in the fridge.

### To cook the lamb and serve

Place lamb on a rack above a roasting dish and cook at 220°C for 25 minutes. If you don't like your lamb quite so pink, cook a further 5–7 minutes. Serve the rack sliced into chops, two bones thick, with fresh greens, grilled aubergine and a generous serving of the marmalade.

## Tips and ideas

- Mix a tablespoon of concentrated pomegranate juice into yoghurt to use as a marinade for lamb or chicken.
- Season duck with the above marinade — it balances the fatty flavours.
- Use concentrated pomegranate juice to flavour the potato filling for samosas.
- Add it to soups — it tastes particularly good in a vegetable chicken broth.
- Jazz up the gravy for a roast of beef.
- Make a walnut dip by puréeing toasted walnuts with spreadable cream cheese, garlic and a dash of concentrated pomegranate juice.
- Add a spoonful or two to a chicken or lamb casserole.
- Toss baby carrots or pan-fried courgettes in a dash of pomegranate juice, the grated rind of an orange and plenty of pepper.

# Port

As history would have it, a dispute between age-old rivals France and England in the eighteenth century served as a catalyst that led to the establishment of the port industry. The relationship between the two nations had deteriorated so much that the British were unable to continue importing claret. The Portuguese solved this problem as the wine they produced in the upper reaches of the spectacular Douro Valley in northern Portugal was just to the British liking.

Since 1756, when Douro became the first wine-growing area to be officially demarcated, port production has been constantly refined. The sheer, terraced, vine-carpeted valley still requires hand-harvesting with each vintage. What a spectacular sight!

And while tradition has played an important part in the history of port, we shouldn't still think of it as only being an after-dinner drink savoured by men.

The rich, fruitier ports, such as Six Grapes (pictured), go well with chocolate, as they are able to stand their ground against its intense flavour. And as they take well to being heated and gently spiced, they're the perfect match to a steamed chocolate pudding.

## Chocolate puddings with spiced port sauce

*Port makes a spectacular sauce to partner a moist and rich chocolate pudding, especially on a winter's night.*

> 250 grams butter
> 250 grams dark chocolate
> 1 tblsp vanilla essence
> 4 eggs
> 4 egg yolks
> ½ cup sugar
> ½ cup flour

### Spiced port sauce
> 2 cups fruity-style port
> 1 vanilla pod, split
> 1 cinnamon stick
> 1 star anise
> ½ cup sugar

### Cook's note
Re-heat the chocolate cakes in the microwave for 1 minute before serving, if wished.

In a saucepan, warm the butter, chocolate and vanilla essence over a low heat until melted. Cool. In a large bowl, beat the eggs and egg yolks until very thick and fluffy.

Sift together the sugar and flour, then fold into the egg mixture with the cooled chocolate mixture. Divide evenly among 8 large, well-greased Texas muffin tins or 16 normal muffin tins. Bake at 190°C for 10–12 minutes until almost cooked. The centre should be a little soft. (Smaller muffins require 8–10 minutes' cooking time.)

Serve warm with the Spiced Port Sauce and whipped cream.

### Spiced port sauce
Place the port, vanilla pod, cinnamon stick and star anise in a saucepan and simmer very slowly until reduced to 1½ cups. Remove the spices and stir in the sugar. Continue to simmer until again reduced to 1½ cups. Cool. The sauce can be prepared in advance.

**Serves 8**

# Prosciutto

Prosciutto is an umbrella name for many different kinds of cured ham. The one we probably know best is Parma ham, which comes from pigs raised in Italy's Emilia-Romagna or Lombardy regions.

Much of the prosciutto we enjoy in New Zealand is imported from Australia. The legs of pork are salted daily for up to a month before they are hung in well-ventilated rooms to dry and mature for over a year.

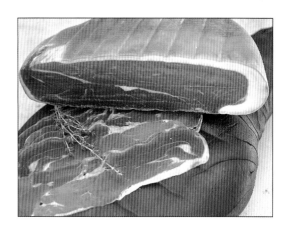

## Marinated leeks with grilled prosciutto

*Prosciutto, salty and chewy, brings marinated autumn leeks to life in this delicious salad, ideal for cooler days.*

4 leeks, washed and trimmed
3/4 cup olive oil
1 tblsp yellow mustard seeds
1 tblsp black mustard seeds
1 tblsp minced fresh garlic
1 bay leaf
2 sprigs thyme
1 cup chicken stock (preferably home-made)
2 tblsp Marsala wine
3 tblsp wine vinegar
salt and pepper to season
8 slices prosciutto

### Salad
radicchio leaves
fresh basil leaves
sundried tomatoes
black olives
crispy fried sourdough bread croutons
caper berries
parmesan cheese, shredded

Cut the leeks into 2 cm thick slices on a slight angle.

Heat 1 tablespoon of the oil in a large frying pan and add the mustard seeds. Cover and cook until they have popped. Add the garlic and cook for 1 minute.

Arrange the leeks on top of the spices, then add the bay leaf and thyme. Pour over the chicken stock and Marsala wine; then cover and simmer gently for 3 minutes. Turn off the heat.

Pour in the remaining olive oil, sprinkle over the wine vinegar and season well with salt and pepper. Cover and refrigerate for 2 hours or up to 3 days.

Grill or pan-fry the prosciutto until crispy. Crumble if wished.

Serve the leeks tossed with a few radicchio and basil leaves and topped with sundried tomatoes, olives, bread croutons, caper berries, parmesan and the crumbled prosciutto.

**Serves 4**

## Tips and ideas
- Serve thin slices wrapped around melon pieces, or folded on their own, as part of an antipasto platter.
- Wrap slices around blanched green vegetables, such as asparagus and beans, and serve with vinaigrette.
- Grill and crumble over pasta, mashed potatoes or polenta.
- Wrap chicken breasts in a slice and layer in a baking dish with a dash of chicken stock, then cover and simmer gently until cooked.
- Add slices to a frittata or pizza.
- Cook and crumble over steamed mussels or pan-fried fish with sundried tomatoes and chopped fresh basil.

# Rose petals

Roses have long been prized for their sweet and heavenly scent, and while they are not a common culinary ingredient, they're one of the most distinguished scents for flavouring food. Subtle, yet luscious and sensual, roses can add sparkle to the simplest of dishes. In the past, roses have been used in sandwiches, made into jams, tossed with cherries in summer puddings and also used in perfumes, toilet waters, hand creams and massage oils. Fragrant rose petals in a recipe can uplift the soul, nourish it, pamper it and refresh it.

## Rose petal shortbread

**250 grams butter (preferably unsalted)**
**¾ cup caster sugar or icing sugar**
**1 or 2 drops rosewater**
**2¼ cups flour**
**¼ cup rice flour**
**1 tsp salt**
**½ cup baby rose petals**

Beat the butter, sugar and rosewater with an electric beater until the mixture is light, fluffy and well creamed. If using caster sugar, the sugar should have dissolved.

Sift the flour, rice flour and salt together and add to the creamed mixture with the rose petals. Stir until the mixture is almost combined.

Turn out onto a floured board. Knead lightly and form into a ball. Roll out gently to a 0.5 cm thickness. Use a cutter to cut into shapes.

Place shortbread onto a baking tray and use fork tines to mark each one three times. Refrigerate 10 minutes or up to 2 hours.

Bake at 160°C for 30–35 minutes, until shortbread is beginning to colour. For darker shortbread, cook a further 5 minutes. Cool on a tray for 10 minutes before transferring to a cake rack. Store in airtight container when cold.

**Makes approximately 35 biscuits**

### Cook's notes

- Make shortbread in a food processor if you don't have a beater, though the butter and sugar cream will not be as light. It is twice as quick though and the end product is still good.
- Rose petals should be dry when adding to shortbread, otherwise they won't adhere to the dough very well.
- Use old-fashioned roses, as they have a definite scent. If using roses that are not strongly perfumed, add a little extra rosewater when creaming butter and sugar.
- Break petals into small pieces so you have bits, not chunks, in the dough.
- If you can, leave the shortbread in an airtight container for 5 days before eating. This will allow the rose flavour to permeate through the shortbread.
- Petals darken on cooking — dark red ones turn black, pink ones browny red.
- Rosewater can be purchased from a good delicatessen or chemist.

### Tips and ideas

- Toss a handful into a summer berry fruit salad.
- Decorate a cream-topped pavlova or sponge with roses.
- Add a couple of handfuls of crushed scented rose petals to a jug of mineral water and stand overnight in the refrigerator before serving.
- Freeze ice-cubes with rose petals and add to drinks.
- Sprinkle rose petals, especially lemon ones, into a summer salad of delicate mesclun greens.
- If you're making mousse or ice cream, infuse the milk or cream with crushed scented rose petals.
- Add clean dry rose petals to strawberry jam just before bottling.
- As an alternative to vanilla sugar, scent caster sugar with roses and use in your baking.

# Rosewater

Distilled from highly perfumed rose petals, rosewater has a heady fragrance and a sweet, exotic taste. Tender babas that have been soaked with rosewater make a different and special after-dinner dessert. Given its intensity, use caution when adding rosewater, and always taste as you go. Cold temperatures mask flavours, so you will need to add more if you use rosewater to flavour a sorbet, ice cream or chilled fruit pudding.

## Rosewater-soaked babas

*Named after the fabled Ali Baba, these yeast cakes are often steeped in rum. Mine are soaked in an orange and rosewater syrup — perfect to serve with fruit.*

### Babas
2½ cups flour
pinch salt
½ cup warm milk
175 grams butter
2–3 tblsp sugar
4 tsp Surebake yeast
4 eggs

### Syrup
2 cups water
1½ cups caster sugar
2–3 tblsp rosewater
juice of 1 orange
grated rind of 1 orange

Sift the flour and salt into a bowl.

Heat together the milk, butter and sugar until lukewarm. Sprinkle over the yeast and stand 5 minutes until frothy.

Beat together the yeast liquid, eggs and flour for five minutes. This is best done using your hands.

Spoon or pipe the mixture into 12 mini rum baba tins. Cover and set aside for 30–40 minutes until double in bulk.

Bake at 200°C for 12–15 minutes until well risen and golden.

Turn out the babas onto a cake rack to cool for 3–5 minutes. Fill a shallow dish with the rosewater syrup.

Soak each baba in the rosewater syrup for 2–3 minutes and then lift out carefully with a slotted spoon. Place on a cake rack. To serve, arrange the babas on plates and fill with whipped cream and fruit of the season.

### Syrup
Put the sugar and water into a saucepan and stir over a moderate heat until the sugar dissolves. Stir in the rosewater, orange juice and rind. Cool to lukewarm.

**Makes 12 babas**

## Tips and ideas

- Sprinkle segments of orange with a few drops of rosewater and a dusting of sugar and serve chilled.
- Flavour a fruit sorbet, purchased or home-made, with rosewater. Combining it with apple, berry fruits or citrus flavours works best.
- Add a few drops to a buttery biscuit recipe.
- In winter, turn a rice pudding into an exotic dessert by adding toasted ground almonds, glacé fruits and a few drops of rosewater.
- In summer, sprinkle strawberries with rose-water and icing sugar or scent a strawberry jelly with a little rosewater.
- Add new interest to a baklava by scenting the sugar syrup with rosewater.
- For a luxurious bath, add plenty of bubble bath and scent with rosewater. Great on a cool spring night.
- Add a few drops to almond oil and rub into your body after that luxurious soak.

# Saffron

Introduced to Spain by the Moors, the finest saffron grows in the parched, colourless plains of La Mancha. Local farmers treat this jewel spice as a cash crop that supplements a rather impoverished income.

The saffron rose (*Crocus sativus*) blossoms in early autumn for two weeks producing tiny purple flowers no higher than 5 cm. The blooms must be picked before the sun rises and the bees visit or the stigmas droop releasing their essential oils. The blooms are taken home to the women who pluck the stigmas from the flowers. The vibrant red/orange stigmas are piled onto plates; it takes all day to collect only a saucerful.

Once the saffron has been dried in a sieve over a gentle charcoal fire, it is kept safely sewn into curtains or tucked in a biscuit tin until it is sold — which could be within weeks, or even years. It takes 160,000 flowers to make 1 kilogram of saffron, worth at least $2000 per kilogram.

When the saffron harvest is over, a celebration is held in the tiny village of Consuegra. Saffron pickers gather to compete for the prestigious title of Dulcinea de La Mancha — the Saffron Queen. Contestants strive to be the one who plucks the saffron rose the fastest and cleanest.

In this area of Spain saffron is an integral part of a life that takes joy in simple pleasures, such as good food. One of Spain's greatest dishes, paella, relies on saffron for its colour and flavour.

## Seafood paella

¼–½ tsp saffron threads
1–2 tsp salt
½ cup dry white wine or dry sherry
¼ cup olive oil
500 grams firm white fish fillets, cut into 3 cm dice
1 medium onion, peeled and finely chopped
1½ cups chopped green and/or red peppers
4 large juicy cloves garlic, peeled and minced
2 tsp paprika
3 large juicy tomatoes, peeled and finely chopped
3 cups short-grain rice
1 bay leaf
5½ cups fish stock
350 grams baby squid, rinsed
6–12 green prawns
6–10 baby-sized green mussels in shell
1 roasted red pepper, finely sliced (optional)
chopped parsley to garnish

Stir the saffron and the salt into the wine. Set aside.

Heat the oil in a paella pan or large wide frying pan until hot. Add the fish pieces and cook until the fish just turns white. Transfer to a plate, cover and set aside in a cool place. Add onions, peppers and garlic to the pan and cook for 3–4 minutes.

Add paprika, tomatoes, rice and bay leaf. Turn to coat rice in the mixture.

Pour the fish stock and saffron-infused wine over the rice. Stir to even out the ingredients and simmer uncovered for 5 minutes. Stir in all the squid, prawns and green mussels. Transfer to a 190°C oven for 10 minutes. Cover with foil and stand on the stove for 10 minutes before serving. Garnish with red peppers if using and with chopped parsley.

**Serves 6**

## Cook's note

You can vary the fish and the seafood in the paella to suit your own tastes and according to what's available. We used snapper and cod. Do it the Spanish way: in the end, stir in some peas with the seafood.

## Tips and ideas

- It's best to buy the saffron in threads, not ground.
- Look for respected names to avoid buying imposters.
- Fake saffron will release its dye instantly while true saffron needs to be soaked before releasing a golden colour.
- Keep saffron in a small airtight container away from light and heat.
- Try saffron in poached pears, breads and cakes.
- Look for Spanish saffron from La Mancha — it is acclaimed as the world's finest.

# Sage

The pungency of sage can verge on the overpowering but, used in moderation, this herb is culinary magic. The oil in sage is so strong that even the dried herb will add a great savoury oomph. Fresh from the garden, the deeply veined, slightly grey leaves are wonderful added whole to casseroles, sprinkled over roasted potatoes or stuffed inside a chicken for roasting. Try chopped sage over a winter soup or stirred into macaroni cheese.

Sage aids with the digestion of rich foods such as roast pork. Just add a little of the herb to an accompanying apple sauce or stuffing. If you love mashed potatoes with parsley, experiment with a little grated onion and chopped fresh sage — sensational and easy.

## Sage and blue cheese sablés

*The natural affinity between sage and mild blue cheddar turns these savoury shortbreads into a memorable and easily made nibble. They are ideal served plain with drinks or accompanying dip, pâté or cheese.*

> **250 grams very cold butter**
> **250 grams blue cheddar cheese (see Cook's note)**
> **250 grams (2 scant level cups) flour**
> **about 10–12 sage leaves**

Grate the butter and cheese in a food processor. Add the flour and sage and process until the mixture forms small moist crumbs.

Turn out and bring the mixture together. Knead gently.

Roll out on a lightly-floured board to about 1/2 cm thick and cut into rounds about 6 cm in diameter. Or use whatever cutter you prefer. Place on baking paper-lined trays.

Bake at 200°C for 15 minutes or until brown and crispy. Cool on a wire cake rack and store in an airtight container. Serve just warm for the best flavour.

**Makes about 30 sablés**

## Cook's notes

- In this recipe, I used Mainland's Blue Cheddar Cheese.
- For a more golden colour, you can brush the sablés with beaten egg before baking.
- These cheese sablés freeze well, either cooked or uncooked. For the uncooked dough, roll into a tight log shape about 4–6 cm in diameter, wrap securely in greaseproof paper, then plastic wrap and freeze. Cut into 1/2 cm slices with a hot knife and bake as above, allowing an extra 2–3 minutes' cooking time.

# Salt

Salt is not only indispensable to good food and good cooking, it is essential to life — although the quantity we require could be debated. Salt is now taking culinary fashion's centre stage, but this is not its first appearance in the limelight. We are but reinventing an ancient wheel.

In times past, salt was exchanged as money. In Roman days soldiers were paid a special allowance — called a salarium — to buy salt. Hence the word salary.

Ancient roads were built for the transportation of salt; the earliest taxes recorded were levied on salt; military campaigns were launched to secure it and even children were sold into slavery for it. Venice, the commercial capital of the ancient world, traded first in salt before spices, cloth and gold.

There should be no apologies for using salt in food. What is sad is that with the overactive promotion of a salt-free diet, a whole generation of cooks knows nothing of how to use this seasoning or how it works to enhance food or preserve it. Try pasta that's not cooked in salt water and, regardless of what you toss it in afterwards, the taste will be disappointing. The same goes for porridge, couscous and bread, which won't rise well without salt. We no longer know not to add salt before cooking legumes and that a pinch of salt added to chilled water will help freshen fish before it's cooked.

Thank goodness then for salt's revival. Now we not only have flaky sea salt to add to focaccia, but we can choose salt from many countries — a touch of Essex, a pinch from Sicily, a grind from New Zealand. If you thought salt was salt, then think again. The trend is just catching on.

## Spiced cold roast fillet of beef with ginger noodle salad

    ½ cup brown sugar
    ½ cup flaky sea salt, like Maldon (see Cook's note)
    1 tsp Chinese five spice mix
    1 tsp ground laos (see Cook's note)
    1 tsp minced fresh ginger
    1 tsp minced garlic
    grated rind of 1 lime
    2 tblsp Indonesian soy sauce
    ¼ cup sherry
    1 tblsp sesame oil
    750 gram piece beef fillet, trimmed
    1–2 tblsp oil

In a bowl, mix together the sugar, flaky sea salt, Chinese five spice, laos, ginger, garlic, lime rind, soy sauce, sherry and sesame oil.

Place the trimmed beef into a deep dish and rub over the marinade. Cover and refrigerate overnight or for 12 hours. Turn the meat. Cover and refrigerate a further 12 hours. Rinse well and pat dry. Alternatively, marinate in a snap-lock bag.

Heat oil in a frying pan until very hot. Seal the beef quickly on all sides. Transfer to a 220°C oven for 15 minutes only.

Cool, wrap in foil and refrigerate 4 hours until cold. Serve sliced over Ginger Noodle Salad.

**Serves 6**

### Cook's notes
- For the beef fillet recipe, use only flaky sea salt. Iodised or free-flowing salt is not recommended here.
- Laos or galangal is a member of the ginger family and can be found in Asian stores or good supermarkets. It is also called Thai ginger. Substitute dried ginger.

### Ginger noodle salad
    250 grams noodles
    2 tblsp oil
    2 cups radicchio leaves, finely shredded
    3 spring onions, finely shredded
    2 tsp minced fresh ginger
    8–10 mangetout, finely shredded
    ¼ cup fresh mint, chopped
    ½ cup walnuts, chopped
    2 tblsp sesame oil
    juice of ½ lemon
    salt and pepper

Cook the noodles in boiling salted water until al dente. Drain well.

Heat the oil in a large frying pan and quickly toss the radicchio leaves, spring onions, ginger and mangetout until all are wilted.

In a bowl, mix together the noodles, vegetables, mint, walnuts, sesame oil, lemon juice and salt and pepper.

# Sherry

Real sherry, made on the south-western coast of Spain, is one of my favourite beverages. Three Moorish towns — Sanlucar de Barrameda, El Puerto de Santa Maria and Jerez de la Fontera — form the triangular boundary where the sherry grapes flourish in chalky soils.

The coastal town of Sanlucar de Barrameda is also famous as the point from which Columbus sailed to find the New World. At El Puerto de Santa Maria we visited the bodegas of Emilio Lustau who produces Almacenista sherries. These sherries are unique and, if you enjoy fine sherry, well worth sampling.

An 'almacenista' (the name means stockholder) buys in sherry and then stores and matures it in his own personal bodega. Creating these fine sherries is a labour of love for many people who also hold down full-time employment elsewhere. Once matured the sherries are transferred to the Emilio Lustau Bodega in Jerez de la Fontera where they are bottled and shipped.

While in Jerez, our favourite town in Spain, we stopped to dine at Bodega la Andana where chef Manuel Valencia Lazo prepared fish with carrot sauce. It was simply divine and I have tried faithfully to re-create it here. Serve with chilled fino for a wonderful meal.

## John Dory with sherry and carrot sauce

4 medium-sized sweet carrots
4 tblsp cream (double cream is best)
½ large or 1 medium-sized onion
4 tblsp olive oil
2 small cloves garlic, crushed and minced
¼ tsp grated nutmeg
¼ cup fino sherry
¾ cup fish stock or carrot cooking water
pinch salt, pepper and sugar to season
4 John Dory fillets
butter
1 tsp finely minced oregano

Peel all the carrots. Chop three of the carrots roughly and simmer gently in boiling salted water until tender. Drain, reserving the water. Purée the boiled carrots with the cream and sufficient water to make a smooth sauce. Keep warm.

Dice the remaining carrot and onion very finely. Heat the oil in a saucepan and cook the onion and garlic over a very low heat until soft but not coloured. Add the carrot and cook a further two minutes. Add the nutmeg and sherry and reduce the heat by half. Add the stock or cooking water and simmer for 2 minutes. Season with salt, pepper and sugar.

Pan-fry the fish in a little butter until just cooked. Add the oregano to the diced carrot sauce.

Divide the sauce evenly between four plates. Place the fish on top of the sauce. Serve with a generous spoonful of carrot purée and vegetables in season.

**Serves 4**

# Sherry vinegar

Sherry vinegar is the rich, aromatic sweet vinegar that comes from Jerez in Spain. It is made with the 'must' (the first pressing) of Palomino grapes, which are used to make fino sherry, and is then left to mature for six years. Like a good vintage wine, the vinegar develops a more complex flavour as it ages. Wonderful in Spanish food, sherry vinegar enhances and seasons the Roasted Gazpacho Soup (below), rather than acting as an acidifier. Sprinkle over hot vegetables and add it to salad dressings and marinades; you can also splash a little into a pan to deglaze it after browning meat. Use sparingly — it is more intense than other wine vinegars.

## Roasted gazpacho soup

*Gazpacho is one of my favourite summer soups. Roasting the vegetables intensifies the naturally sweet flavours. Traditionally, it is eaten icy cold but I prefer to serve it cool, at room temperature.*

    1 small red onion, peeled and cut into 8 wedges
    6 large ripe tomatoes, cut in half horizontally
    1 yellow pepper, deseeded and cut into 4 strips
    1 red pepper, deseeded and cut into 4 strips
    4–5 cloves garlic, skins on
    1 tblsp olive oil
    ½ cucumber, peeled and deseeded
    2 tblsp fresh basil
    2 cups tomato juice
    3 tblsp extra-virgin olive oil
    2 tblsp sherry vinegar

### Salsa garnish
    ½ small red onion, finely chopped
    5 cm piece cucumber, peeled, deseeded and finely chopped
    1 large ripe tomato, skinned, deseeded and chopped (see Cook's note)
    1 tblsp fresh basil

Arrange red onion wedges, tomato halves, yellow and red pepper strips and garlic on a foil-lined baking tray. Brush with 1 tablespoon oil and season with salt and pepper. Cook at 200°C for 20–25 minutes or until tender and the edges of the vegetables are just beginning to brown.

Reserve 2 pepper strips for garnish. Remove garlic skins, then put the remaining roasted vegetables in a food processor with cucumber, basil and half the tomato juice and blend until smooth (you may have to do this in two batches if your processor bowl is small).

Gradually stir in remaining tomato juice and olive oil to give a soupy consistency. Season with sherry vinegar, adding more salt and pepper as necessary. Cool or chill.

Serve the soup sprinkled with the Salsa garnish and garlicky croutons or grissini sticks.

### Salsa garnish
Dice reserved roasted pepper strips and combine with red onion, cucumber, tomato and basil.

**Serves 4–5**

### Cook's note
Place the tomato in a bowl and pour over boiling water. Lift out with a slotted spoon, the skin will peel away easily. Cut in half horizontally and squeeze out the seeds.

# Sichuan peppercorns

If you enjoy the flavours of spicy Chinese food, then you'll love using Sichuan peppercorns. They come from a deciduous tree, the prickly ash, and when dried the reddish-brown berries split to reveal tiny black seeds.

The peppercorns have a warm, peppery and fragrant aroma with citrus notes and, when you crush them in your hands, you can smell lavender flowers. They add tang to your Chinese cooking and are wonderful to have on hand in the kitchen.

You can buy dried whole peppercorn berries from good Asian food shops and some supermarkets. Often the berries will still have tiny thorns left on them. These need to be picked out before cooking.

Good spice brands use Sichuan peppercorns in their five-spice powder blends. Read the side of the packet before buying — the inclusion of these peppercorns helps create a superior blend.

The spicy flavour of Sichuan peppercorns make them a great partner for pork or duck and with salty foods. Blended with salt, you can rub Sichuan peppercorns into pork chops or chicken breasts before barbecuing, though be careful not to use too much heat when cooking as dried spices burn easily.

Look out, too, for sancho powder — it is the crushed dried leaf of the Sichuan pepper tree.

## Spicy Sichuan duck

> 1 tblsp Sichuan peppercorns
> grated rind and juice of 2 oranges
> 1 tblsp honey or brown sugar
> ¼ cup Grand Marnier
> ½ tsp salt
> 4 duck leg and thigh portions
> pared rind of 2 oranges
> 2–3 tblsp balsamic vinegar
> ¼ cup virgin olive oil
> 1 tblsp honey
> salt and pepper

Process Sichuan peppercorns, orange rind and juice, honey or sugar, Grand Marnier and salt in a food processor or crush together in a mortar and pestle.

Place duck portions into a shallow dish and pour over the peppercorn mix, turning to coat evenly. Cover and refrigerate overnight.

Heat a non-stick frying pan with 1 tablespoon oil and, when very hot, place in the duck portions, skin side down. Cook over a moderately high heat for 2 minutes until the skin is nicely browned. Turn over and repeat.

Transfer the duck to an ovenproof dish and cook in an oven at 180°C for 45 minutes.

To make the dressing, add the orange peel to the frying pan and cook over a moderate heat until it is slightly crispy. Add the balsamic vinegar and stir to deglaze the pan. Mix with the oil and honey and season the dressing with salt and pepper.

To serve, place the duck on your favourite salad greens and top with the warm balsamic honey dressing.

**Serves 4**

# Smoked paprika

Christopher Columbus is credited with introducing capsicums (from which we obtain paprika) to Spain way back in 1493. But it was not until 1993 that the Spaniards produced smoked paprika. Hailing from La Vera in Extremadura in western Spain, smoked paprika is sensational, extremely different to ordinary paprika. The peppers are slowly smoked over oak ash before being stoneground for about eight hours to become a fine powder. It is best to cook the paprika in a dash of oil before mixing to allow the flavours to be unlocked.

### Three styles

**Dulce** (sweet). Great with potatoes, rice and fish dishes.
**Agridulce** (bittersweet). Use in meat, bean and game dishes.
**Picante** (spicy hot). Not as hot as it sounds and my favourite. Try it
with strongly-flavoured garlic dishes.

## Smoked pumpkin chutney

*Pumpkins are available all year round and this chutney makes a great change to have with cold meats.*

2 bulbs garlic
1 kg firm-fleshed pumpkin (crown or buttercup)
¼ cup oil
2 onions, peeled and finely chopped
2 large red chillies, deseeded and chopped
1 tblsp chopped lemon grass
1 tblsp bittersweet smoked paprika
1 tblsp salt
2 cups cider vinegar
1½ cups white sugar

Place the garlic bulbs in baking paper or foil and drizzle with a little oil. Wrap securely and cook at 180°C for 35–40 minutes or until a skewer can be easily inserted. Cool.

Peel and very finely dice the pumpkin.

Heat the oil in a large preserving pan and cook the onion, chillies and lemon grass until they are soft but not brown. Add the bittersweet smoked paprika and cook a further minute.

Cut the garlic bulbs in half and squeeze the pulp into the pan. Add the pumpkin, salt, vinegar and sugar and simmer gently for 15 minutes until the chutney is thick and pulpy.

Spoon into hot, sterilised jars. Cool, seal and label.

Variation: add ½ cup chopped raisins or sultanas with the pumpkin.

**Makes 4 x 350 ml bottles**

# Star anise

Delicate and beautiful, star anise is the exceptionally fragrant dried fruit of a tree (*Illicium verum*) native to southern China. Each of the eight uneven points of the spice encase a little brown seed. It is best to buy whole spices as the seeds are not as flavoursome as the rest of the pod.

Star anise is a key ingredient in five-spice powder and its liquorice-like flavour adds a sweet note to pork, beef, chicken and winter vegetables. Its warming properties are perfect at colder times of the year.

## Star anise-scented winter pork casserole

750 grams lean shoulder pork
¼ cup flour
½ tsp each ground five-spice powder, pepper and salt
about ¼ cup oil
2 cups chicken stock
¼ cup sweet sherry
500 grams golden kumara, peeled and sliced
500 grams pumpkin, peeled and diced
1 star anise
2 onions, peeled and diced
2 tblsp brown sugar
3 courgettes, trimmed and sliced

Cut pork into 3 cm pieces. Mix together flour, five spice, pepper and salt. Toss pork in seasoned flour; shake to remove excess. Brown pork in half the oil in a hot frying pan. Transfer to a 2-litre casserole. Add stock and sherry to frying pan. Boil, scraping sediment from the pan into the stock.

Add stock to the casserole with the kumara, pumpkin and star anise. Cover and simmer for 45 minutes over a moderate heat on top of the stove or in a 180°C oven.

Heat the remaining oil in a clean frying pan and cook the onions over a moderate heat until they are well browned. Add the brown sugar; toss to glaze the onions.

Add the onions and courgettes to the casserole and cook a further 20 minutes until the courgettes and pork are tender. Serve with creamy mashed potatoes.

**Serves 6**

## Tips and ideas

If you like five-spice powder, try this recipe. (You'll need a coffee mill to grind the spices fine enough.)

3 star anise
1 tblsp Sichuan pepper
½ cinnamon stick
1 tblsp fennel seeds
½ tblsp whole cloves

Place all ingredients in a coffee mill and grind until very fine. For a more fragrant mix, add 3–4 whole cardamom pods.

# Sumac

As a nation we're not great lovers of tart flavours, but there's no better way to give summer fare a bit of a kick. Enter sumac — a traditional Middle Eastern seasoning that offers zesty flavour without the acidity of lemon or vinegar. The deep-crimson-coloured berries are more commonly sold finely ground and used as a spice. Mixed with salt, sumac acts as a preservative or, added to salt and oil, it brings moistness and flavour to food. The whole berries can be soaked in water to make a refreshing, sour drink.

Sprinkle sumac on grilled lamb or beef, boiled new potatoes, grilled fish, a warm spinach-style salad or over sliced avocados before serving, to add colour and interest to the dish. Or try keeping a bowl of ground sumac on the table along with salt and pepper to give your food instant life.

In ancient times, when lemons weren't known, sumac was commonly used. Today it can be found in most specialty cook-shops, particularly those that stock Middle Eastern products. When buying, look for powder that has an even colour and texture, and make sure you store it away from light and moisture.

## Spiced slow-roasted tomatoes on Turkish bread

*Great for brunch, these tomatoes can be cooked in advance and then warmed in a low oven when required.*

**12–16 medium-sized tomatoes**
**1 tblsp caster sugar**
**2–3 tsp crushed salt flakes**
**freshly ground black pepper**
**2–3 tsp ground sumac**
**¼ cup olive oil**

Halve the tomatoes and place in a lasagne-style dish.
Sprinkle over the sugar, salt flakes, pepper and sumac.
Drizzle with the olive oil.
Roast at 140°C for 1½ hours until the tomatoes have shrunk slightly but are not burnt or dried.
Serve the tomatoes on warmed pide (Turkish) bread with crumbled feta cheese and chopped fresh mint. Drizzle on extra olive oil if wished.

**Serves 6**

# Tamarind

The rather unusual, if not ugly features of tamarind, belie its wonderful souring properties. Also known as the Indian Date (due to that country's large use of the spice), tamarind has been around for centuries. It's the key ingredient in Worcestershire sauce and was used in ancient medicine as a tonic for good liver and kidney function, to cure upset stomachs and quench thirst.

The tamarind tree bears long brown pods, which, when cracked, open to reveal a sticky red-brown pulp and as many as 10 seeds. The pulp, along with the outside pods, seeds and fibrous matter is then dried and packaged up for export.

Tamarind is sold in dark-brown solid blocks. You'll find it in supermarkets and Asian or Indian food shops. It will keep for 12 months well wrapped in the refrigerator.

## Prawns in sweet hot curry

3 tsp tamarind pulp
1 cup warm water
3 large onions, peeled and finely chopped
½ cup oil, a light olive is best
4–6 green or red chillies, deseeded and finely sliced
6 large juicy cloves garlic, crushed, peeled and mashed to a paste
1 ½ tsp each ground coriander and chilli powder
2 tsp ground cumin
2 tsp garam masala
1 tsp ground turmeric
4 large juicy tomatoes, blanched, peeled and finely diced
1 tsp brown sugar
½ cup coriander leaves
1 tsp salt
500 grams shelled and deveined green prawns

Break up the tamarind pulp, place in the warm water and set aside for 20 minutes. Squash the softened tamarind pulp with your fingers or a heavy spoon until the water is murky and you are left only with seeds and fibre. Strain the tamarind and reserve the water.

Cook the onion in the oil in a large frying pan over a moderately hot heat for about 20 minutes, stirring regularly until the onion is well browned but not burnt. Add the sliced chilli, garlic and dried spices (coriander, chilli, cumin, garam masala and turmeric) and cook a further minute.

Add the tomatoes, brown sugar, coriander leaves, tamarind water and salt and stir over a moderate heat for 10 minutes until the mixture is thick and pulpy.

Add prawns and cook, turning over a moderate heat for 10 minutes until they're cooked. Don't over-cook. The prawns should be a soft pink colour. Serve with rice and poppadums.

**Serves 4**

# Turmeric

It is knobbly, rustic, even ugly looking, yet turmeric's appearance belies a pleasing warm and unique flavour that cannot really be replaced by any other spice. Ground turmeric is sold in two types — Madras and Allepey — both named after places in India. If possible, purchase the latter. Its flavour is superior. Fresh turmeric is now available here in specialty spice and Asian food stores. Look for firm, clean, knobbly rhizomes (roots) and store them at home in the onion or potato bin, somewhere with fresh, circulating air. Turmeric should last about two weeks. Once used as a dye, it stains badly so be sure to wear rubber gloves when preparing it. Use turmeric as you would fresh ginger: grated or sliced.

## Sweet cucumber pickle

**1.75 kg (about 4) short cucumbers**
**600 grams (about 4 large) onions**
**6 tblsp salt (not iodised or flaky)**
**about 8 cups ice-cold water to cover**
**1 litre cider or white-wine vinegar**
**1 tblsp ground turmeric**
**1 tblsp mustard seeds**
**2 tsp white peppercorns**
**18 whole cloves**
**¼ tsp celery seed (optional)**
**3½ cups sugar**

Cut the cucumbers and onions into 2 mm thick slices and layer in a deep non-metallic bowl with the salt and then pour over the ice-cold water. Cover and allow to stand in a cold place (a refrigerator is best) overnight.

Drain well the next day, rinse thoroughly in fresh cold water and drain again.

Place in a large saucepan or preserving pan with the vinegar, turmeric, mustard seeds, peppercorns, cloves, celery seeds if using and sugar. Bring to a rapid boil. Continue boiling for 10 minutes, stirring occasionally.

Bottle in hot sterilised jars and seal. Stand 2 weeks, if you can, before serving.

**Makes 2.5 litres**

## Tips and ideas

- Add to spice mixes where you want a warm, earthy flavour. Curries are lost without it. Madras turmeric is used in most curry powders and has more colour than flavour. Add a bit more for extra taste.
- Add to rice — either pilaf or boiled — to add colour and flavour.
- Add a little to cheese shortbreads or other savoury biscuits, cheese breads or scones.
- Use in pickles and chutneys with mangoes, pawpaws, cucumbers, onions, aubergines and chokos.

# Vanilla

Vanilla is the pod of the *Vanilla planifolia* orchid, the only orchid of 20,000 varieties to produce something edible. Vanilla originated in Mexico, where the Aztecs used it to heighten the taste of a flavoured chocolate drink. Mexico held the monopoly on vanilla production until 1841, when artificial fertilisation of the plant by hand was developed.

Vanilla pods are the best way of using vanilla. The pods can be used whole to flavour syrups and sauces or can be split and the seeds included in the dish. This will ensure a more intense flavour. The finest vanilla pods come with a coating of white crystals. This is the natural vanillin, which gives vanilla its characteristic flavour. Vanilla pods can also be re-used. Wash them well to remove any syrup or milk and let them dry out in a warm place, such as on a kitchen windowsill. Store vanilla pods in an airtight jar, away from direct sunlight.

Imitation vanilla essence is artificially made, mainly using by-products of the paper industry. It has a harsh taste, so you're better off buying pure vanilla essence. These two products sit side by side in the stores.

## Panna cotta

*All the seeds from one vanilla pod are used to make this delicious Italian cream dessert.*

> 1 vanilla pod
> 1½ cups double cream
> pared rind of 1 lemon
> ½ cup caster sugar
> 2 tsp gelatin
> 2 tblsp almond liqueur (Amaretto)
> ¾ cup standard cream
> seasonal poached fruits to accompany

Split vanilla pod lengthways and scoop out the seeds.

Place the seeds in a saucepan with the double cream, lemon rind and caster sugar, then slowly bring to the boil. Strain to remove the lemon rind.

Sprinkle the gelatin over the liqueur and leave to swell. Dissolve by standing over a bowl of hot water or placing in the microwave on full power for 15–20 seconds. Pour the gelatin into the hot double cream and stir well to mix. Cover and set aside in the refrigerator until the cream has almost set.

Whip the standard cream to soft peaks and fold into the double cream mixture. Spoon into 6 x ¾ cup moulds and refrigerate for at least 4 hours or, ideally, overnight. To turn out the moulds, run a hot cloth around the outside of the moulds and turn onto a plate. Hold the plate and mould together and give a good shake to release the dessert. Serve with poached fruits.

### Cook's note

Don't apply too much heat to the moulds, as panna cotta melts easily. If you can't find double cream, look for one that contains at least 43–48 percent fat.

**Serves 6**

## Tips and ideas

- Add a pod or two to a potpourri mix. Particularly pleasant in the bathroom or bedroom.
- Infuse double cream with vanilla pods before serving over a winter steamed pudding.
- Add a vanilla pod to poached fruit. It goes well with stone and berry fruits.
- Add a pod to your sugar or caster sugar container to permeate and create vanilla sugar. Use vanilla sugar in all your baking.
- Add seeds to baked custard, creamed rice, crème brûlée, crème caramel and similar custard dishes.
- Always make sure that you add pure vanilla essence to your chocolate baking and desserts. It really does enhance the flavour of chocolate. It's also great with coffee.
- Vanilla is considered an aphrodisiac, which may be why many perfumes contain it. If you use massage oils, add a few seeds to infuse the oil. It's also said to be consoling in times of stress.
- If you are cleaning out the refrigerator or have a plastic container that smells, add a few drops of imitation vanilla essence to the final rinsing water. It will help refresh the container.

# Verjuice

Slightly sharp, slightly sour, verjuice is commonly made from the juice of unripe grapes but can also be made from crab apples and apples. Verjuice should be enjoyed young and fresh, preferably in the year of its vintage. Left to age, it can oxidise, taking on appley characteristics. Its flavour will depend on the apple or grape variety, the season and the ripeness of the fruit when picked.

Use verjuice where you would use a light vinegar (such as cider or white wine) or a dash of vinegar. Taste your verjuice first so that you can assess its flavours and how much to use. Avoid pairing it with pungent flavours or overpowering spices as its delicate taste will be lost.

## Seared duck with watercress salad and verjuice dressing

### Duck

**2 double duck breasts**
**sea salt**
**ground black pepper**
**2 tblsp verjuice**
**2 tblsp chopped fresh chervil or parsley**
**350 grams baby new potatoes, cooked and cold**
**8 artichoke hearts, quartered**
**¼ cup pinenuts**
**4 handfuls watercress**
**100 grams grapes, halved**

### Verjuice dressing

**2 tblsp verjuice**
**squeeze of lemon juice**
**2 tblsp olive oil**
**juice from the duck**
**2 tblsp chopped fresh herbs (chervil)**
**salt and pepper**

Score the duck fat in a diamond pattern and season the fat side well with salt and pepper. Heat a frying pan until very hot and add the duck fat-side down. Cook for 3 minutes each side.

Place the duck breasts on a plate, pour over the verjuice and sprinkle over the chervil or parsley. Cover and set aside for 3 minutes. (Keep the juice that collects on the plate). Add the potatoes to the fat in the pan and cook over a moderately-high heat until browned. Add the artichoke hearts and pinenuts to the pan and toss quickly to brown and heat through.

Prepare the dressing. In a clean bowl, mix together the verjuice, lemon juice, olive oil, reserved juice from the rested duck and chervil. Season with salt and pepper. Slice the duck on an angle into thin slices, then arrange the potatoes, pinenuts, artichokes, grapes and watercress on serving plates and fan the duck breast on top. Pour over the dressing and serve immediately.

**Serves 4**

## Tips and ideas

- Add a dash to poached fruit to balance the sweetness.
- Make a delicious dressing by combining equal quantities of verjuice, walnut oil and honey.
- Use 1 or 2 tablespoons to deglaze a pan after pan-frying chicken, fish or seafood.
- Toss summer fruit salsas with verjuice — it's not as sharp as vinegar.
- Make a syrup with equal quantities verjuice to water. Add a little lemon rind or a cardamom pod or two and simmer for 15 minutes. Skim and serve with poached fruit.
- If you make a sauce to accompany seafood, add a dash of verjuice to give it a wonderful lift.
- Verjuice can be purchased from good delicatessens.

# Vietnamese mint

With our greater awareness and enjoyment of Asian foods, Vietnamese mint is becoming increasingly popular. The long, thin, tapering, dark green leaves are smudged black in places and have an intensely minty, citrus flavour with a chilli-like afterkick. Beware, a little is enough.

This interestingly named plant is not a mint at all — it is a polygonum and is related to sorrel. It will grow well in tubs or boxes and, like mint, can be prolific so keeping it contained in a box is a good idea.

Keep Vietnamese mint as you do other herbs: wash in cold water, shake off the excess and place in a snap-lock bag in the fridge.

## Vietnamese minted beef salad

400 grams lean beef fillet
2 tblsp chopped fresh basil
2 tblsp chopped fresh coriander, with stalk if possible
2 tblsp chopped fresh Vietnamese mint
2 tsp minced fresh garlic
2 tsp minced fresh chilli
2 tblsp olive oil
2 carrots, peeled and finely sliced
100 grams mangetouts, sliced (optional)
50 grams cellophane noodles
½ telegraph cucumber, deseeded and sliced
1 mango, peeled and finely sliced

### Dressing

2 tsp minced fresh ginger
1 tsp minced fresh chilli
1 tblsp caster sugar
½ lime, quartered, deseeded and chopped
1½ tblsp fish sauce
½ cup water
2 tblsp chopped Vietnamese mint

## Tips and ideas
- Add it chopped to a chicken laksa or clear chicken and corn soup.
- Add torn leaves to Asian salads.
- Add to spring rolls.
- Use it to jazz up a Chinese stir-fry or takeaway.
- Add a few leaves to a spicy salsa or pesto.

Cut the beef into thin strips and place in a bowl with the basil, coriander, Vietnamese mint, garlic, chilli and oil, then toss to marinate. Stand covered for 20 minutes.

Blanch the carrots and the mangetouts quickly. Refresh in cold water and drain.

Soak the cellophane noodles in boiling water for 20 minutes until tender and then cut into 10 cm lengths. Drain well on a clean cloth.

Heat a frying pan and cook the beef over a high heat for about 3–4 minutes until well browned and just cooked.

Toss the beef, vegetables, mango slices and the noodles together with the dressing.

To make the dressing, put the ginger, chilli, sugar, lime, fish sauce, water and Vietnamese mint into a blender. Process to make a smooth sauce.

**Serves 4**

# Walnut oil

Light and heady with a sweet youthful flavour, walnut oil is sensational to have on hand, breathing new life into simple dishes such as mashed potatoes. Locally, this fledgling industry is growing up around the main wine districts — Marlborough, Canterbury, Central Otago, Hawke's Bay and Martinborough. To enliven your food, seek out local walnut oil — unlike many imported products, it's so wonderfully fresh, you'll be an instant convert.

### How it's made
Walnuts are picked from selected trees and only the finest are used for oil. The nut is cracked and the meat ground to a paste but, unlike with overseas walnut oils, the nut is not roasted as heating destroys many of the nutrients.

The churned mass or paste is then placed on mats and, when pressed, the light-coloured oil runs freely. The oil is left to settle before being decanted into dark glass bottles, which help protect it from light.

The nuts are cracked for oil on demand. The date of crushing is shown on the bottle and the oil must be used within 12 months. This practice has been established by New Zealand producers 'A Cracker of a Nut' to avoid any chance of rancidity.

## Autumn mashed potatoes

> 1 kg starchy potatoes
> 1 tsp salt
> ½ tsp white pepper
> about ¼ cup walnut oil
> milk
> 4 rashers streaky bacon, finely sliced
> 1 onion, peeled and finely sliced
> ½ cup walnuts

Peel the potatoes and place in cold water. Bring to the boil and then simmer for 15 minutes or until the potatoes are tender when tested with a skewer or knife.

Drain and mash the potatoes well. Season with salt and pepper. Using a fork, whip in the walnut oil and sufficient milk to make smooth mashed potatoes.

Cook the bacon and onion in a dash of oil until well browned. If the bacon has a little fat on it, do not add any more oil to the pan. Stir in the walnuts.

Serve the potatoes in a large bowl garnished with the bacon mix and a pouring of walnut oil.

**Serves 6**

## Tips and ideas
Walnut oil burns when heated in a frying pan, so it's best used for tasting. Try this . . .

- Drizzle over grilled fish or seafood just before serving.
- Toss through pasta with slices of prosciutto, parmesan and fresh parsley.
- Make a sensational dressing using one-third parts lemon juice, honey and walnut oil — it's great over a green salad or even a fruit salad.
- Use instead of olive oil as a dip to serve with bread and dukkah (a spicy Turkish mix).
- Use in place of butter to drizzle over steamed fresh carrots, pumpkin or green beans.
- Using your favourite pecan pie recipe, substitute walnut oil for butter and walnuts for pecans.

# Watercress

When you bite into watercress, you're hit with an explosion of hot, spicy, peppery flavours with refreshing crisp, green notes. Watercress adds wonderful flavour to a simple salad in spring or a hot potato soup in winter. Available almost all year around, it is often seen as a ubiquitous garnish rather than a component to a dish and it partners particularly well with game. Try including the leaves regularly with other vegetables as watercress is also high in vitamins C and A along with calcium and iron. Popular since ancient times, it has also been used as a medical remedy — the Romans even eating the leaves to prevent baldness.

## Spring chicken and cress salad

> 1 smoked chicken
> 250 grams cherry tomatoes, halved
> 2–3 tsp minced fresh ginger
> 1 tsp minced fresh garlic
> 1 tsp minced red chilli
> 6–8 basil leaves
> 2 tblsp chopped fresh mint
> grated rind and juice of 1 lemon
> 2 tblsp cider or white-wine vinegar
> 4 tblsp olive oil
> 2 avocados, stoned, peeled and sliced
> 1 small red onion, peeled and finely sliced
> 3–4 cups watercress leaves
> unsweetened yoghurt, to accompany (optional)

Break the chicken into small bite-size pieces, discarding the skin and bones. Place in a bowl with the cherry tomatoes.

Mix together the ginger, garlic, chilli, basil, mint, lemon juice and rind, vinegar and olive oil and toss with the chicken. Cover and stand for 30 minutes.

Add the sliced avocados, red onion and watercress and toss gently. Serve in bowls soon after making and drizzle with yoghurt if wished.

**Serves 4**

## Tips and ideas
- Look for bright, deep-coloured leaves.
- The stems should be crisp not limp.
- Yellowing on the leaves is a sign of ageing and flavour loss.
- The leaves are used rather than the stems which can be stringy. Chop and use the stems, if wished, for a more pungent flavour.
- Do not over-cook watercress if adding to soups or sauces. It will quickly turn grey and its sweet flavour will be lost to more sour, dank grass notes.
- To keep, rinse in cold water and shake off the excess. Place in a sealed snap-lock bag or wrap in a clean cloth and refrigerate.

# Worcestershire sauce

So often a bottle of Worcestershire sauce sits lost at the back of the pantry, only occasionally asked to breathe life into our cooking. Well, bring it forward! Pungent, aromatic and hot, Worcestershire sauce can be an incredibly valuable addition to so many meals. It will jazz up the humble burger, casserole, gravy, soup, stir-fry or cheese dish.

It is one of the best things to have come from the Brits' time in India. Many of the returning army officers brought back their own recipes for hot, sour, salty sauces and Lea & Perrins Worcestershire sauce has stood the test of time.

There are many romantic stories about its origins but none is more romantic than this one: the sauce was said to have been made in a chemist shop in Worcester, England (Lea & Perrins) but the customer never came to collect it. Therefore it was stored for many years where it possibly fermented and matured. The store owner, on discovering the barrel, tasted it before discarding the contents and, discovering the change from brash sauce to admirable condiment, began to reproduce it.

Worcestershire sauce is now enjoyed the world over and the following version of Welsh Rabbit is a perfect way to savour the flavour regularly.

## Worcestershire rabbit

250 grams (2½ cups) grated tasty cheddar
25 grams butter
2–3 tblsp Worcestershire sauce
¼ cup dark beer
salt and pepper to season
1 cup leftover cold meat (chicken, ham or beef)
4 slices thick white bread or focaccia

Put the cheese, butter, Worcestershire sauce and beer into a saucepan and stir over a low heat until the cheese has melted and the mixture is smooth and creamy. Season with salt and pepper.

Toast the bread under a grill on one side only and then top the ungrilled side with a little of the cold meat.

Spoon an equal amount of the cheese mixture over the top. Grill under a high heat until golden and the cheese is bubbling. Serve immediately.

**Serves 2–4 (depending on appetites)**

## Tips and ideas

- Add to gravy for flavour — especially great with gravy for roast beef.
- Season-up a casserole with a few shakes.
- Toss with mustard and sugar to make a devilled marinade for kidneys.
- Rub over lamb chops before grilling.
- Don't forget to enjoy the occasional spiced Bloody Mary.
- Add to mayonnaise or a hollandaise sauce.
- Add to any beef mince dish for a boost of flavour.
- Shake over pan-fried fish and top with chopped parsley and butter.
- Season winter vegetable soups before serving.
- Serve with curries or stir-fries for a change.
- Bean and lentil dishes are improved with a few shakes.

# Za'atar

Za'atar is an aromatic blend of herbs and spices used across the Middle East. It consists of fresh or dried thyme, sesame seeds, ground sour, red, sumac berries and salt — although the proportions of each can vary. Za'atar's tangy, aromatic flavour goes well with lamb or chicken. Try it on kebabs. Simply brush the meat with olive oil and sprinkle with the spice blend, leave to marinate and then cook on a barbecue or under a hot grill. Serve with hummus or tzatziki, in warm pita bread or with couscous.

Potatoes are delicious mashed with olive oil and za'atar, or add it to cubed potatoes for roasting. Peel and dice 500–700 grams potatoes into 2 cm pieces, toss in a plastic bag with 1 tablespoon olive oil and 1–2 tablespoons za'atar, arrange on an oven tray and cook at 200°C for 30 minutes or until tender, golden and delicious.

## Lebanese flatbreads with za'atar

*In the Lebanese markets they serve mankoushi for breakfast. The flat, round breads are smothered in za'atar and cooked in a wood-fired oven. Try them for lunch served warm with Middle Eastern dips, roasted peppers and cherry tomatoes.*

> 3 tsp dried yeast
> 2 tsp sugar
> 1½ cups warm water
> 3 cups high-grade flour
> 2 tsp salt
> 3 tblsp za'atar
> 5 tblsp olive oil
> flaky sea salt

Mix together yeast, sugar and warm water and set aside for 10 minutes until the mixture is light and frothy.

Sift flour and salt into a large bowl. Make a well in the centre. Add the frothy yeast liquid. Mix together to form a soft dough. Alternatively, mix in a food processor for 1–2 minutes or prepare in a bread maker.

Turn out and knead firmly for 10–12 minutes until the dough is supple. Cover with a clean tea towel and leave for 45–60 minutes until double in bulk.

Deflate the dough gently and cut into 10 equal pieces, shape into buns and roll into rounds about 15 cm in diameter. Place on greased or baking paper-lined trays.

Combine za'atar and oil and brush over flatbreads. Leave to prove in a warm place for a further 10 minutes.

Sprinkle with a little flaked salt. Bake the flatbreads at 200°C for 12–15 minutes until golden and cooked through.

**Makes 10 breads**

## To make za'atar

> 3 tsp crushed dried thyme or 2 tblsp
>    chopped fresh thyme
> 1 tsp sumac
> 1 tsp toasted sesame seeds
> ¼ tsp salt

Combine all ingredients. Store in an airtight container for a few weeks. If adding fresh thyme, use within 1–2 days.

# Trade secrets

For reference, herbs are the leaves of plants that we use to add or enhance flavours in cooking and any other part of the plant, usually dried, is the spice. Spices can be bark (e.g. cinnamon), buds (e.g. cloves), berries (e.g. peppercorns), seeds (e.g. cumin), roots (e.g. ginger) or stigma of flowers (e.g. saffron). Many plants we use as both herbs and spice. The leaves are used in cooking and the spices are gathered once the plant has finished flowering. Coriander is a great example of this.

## Herbs

Herbs can be used fresh or dried, depending on the application and the recipe. Dried herbs often get a 'bad run', but many ancient cultures have used dried herbs in their cooking for centuries.

- Freshness is critical to a herb's good flavour — whether dried or fresh. Dried herbs kept too long in a pantry cupboard lose their flavour. I always write the purchase date on the packets so I know how old they are and after a year I tend to replace them.
- As dried herbs are a concentrated form of the herb, use sparingly and if substituting dried for fresh, use about $\frac{1}{4}$–$\frac{1}{2}$ depending on the dish.
- To tell if dried herbs are still at their best, rub a little in your hands and if they have a pleasant aroma they should be fine. If they are musty throw them away.
- Do not leave fresh herbs damp in plastic bags or foam trays as they will sweat, become mouldy and the 'off' flavours are easily absorbed.
- I keep fresh herbs in the fridge the following way: wash herbs and place stems down in a plastic bag, with only the water that clings to their leaves. Blow the bag up with your breath and tie with a wire twist tie to seal. Repeat daily.
- Gently-scented herbs such as chervil should be kept separate from strongly-scented herbs such as basil to ensure no cross-over of flavour.
- How you chop herbs is up to you. For ease I use a chopping board and a cook's knife, however, scissors or a herb chopper are just fine.

## Spices

Spices, although dried, also need to be fresh. Open a packet of freshly-grated nutmeg and have a deep indulgent sniff of the intoxicating aroma. If old, there is no such smell and it's easy to tell that the spice is past its use-by-date.

- Most whole spices will keep for up to three years if stored in an airtight container. Ground spices will last about 12 months. Always keep in airtight containers and away from moisture, excessive heat (e.g. beside the stove) and direct sunlight.
- Whole spices are great to cook with, but often it is difficult to find them, as supermarkets predominantly sell ground spices. Check out Indian and Asian food stores for whole spices. Freshly ground spices are wonderful to work with: I grind mine in a coffee bean grinder that I keep especially for the purpose.
- In some cultures spices are toasted or fried, often with other ingredients such as onions, before the wet ingredients are added. For example, spices in Sri Lankan curries are cooked or fried longer than curries from northern India. This cooking process gives the spices a different flavour to those that have just been added to a sauce as you make it. Spice mixes such as garam masala are often pre-toasted and stirred in just before serving to give a different depth of flavour. So be creative with how you use spices in your cooking.

## Oils and flavourings

Oils should also be fresh. Rancid oils impart a bitter and unpleasant flavour to foods. The best way to buy oil is in cans, then decant it into a smaller container for everyday use.

- Make sure you seal the lid well after decanting.
- Keep oils away from heat and direct light as these hasten the rancidity process.
- If your requirements are small, buy only as required and store in a cool cupboard.
- Flavourings such as rosewater or orange water will last indefinitely. Use sparingly as they can be overpowering.

# Index

# Index